Advance Praise for
Slow Down, Sell Faster!

"Salespeople involved in today's high-value, complex sale will find that Kevin Davis' book provides exactly what they need to know to close the deal. This book provides solid, practical advice that professional salespeople can immediately use and apply."
—Stephen J. Bistritz, Ed.D., President and Founder, SellXL.com; co-author of *Selling to the C-Suite*

"The need to be more *buyer*-focused is clear to most all Chief Sales Officers; how to do it is not. In *Slow Down, Sell Faster!* Kevin Davis offers a concise roadmap for how to stop paying lip service to this concept and make it a reality for sales reps and their managers."
—Jim Dickie, Managing Partner, CSO Insights

"As the provider of choice for our customers' business technology needs it is imperative that we have a sales process focused on the customer buying cycle. Years ago, we selected Kevin Davis' sales model. We've used the flexibility of the program to train the majority of our sales force on this powerful consultative selling methodology. We've measured outstanding results."
—Dan Cooper, Executive VP, Field Operations, Xerox, Global Imaging Systems

SLOW DOWN, SELL FASTER!

Bob,

If we focus on the success of our customers, our success will naturally follow.

Enjoy the read!

SLOW DOWN, SELL FASTER!

Understand Your Customer's Buying Process and Maximize Your Sales

Kevin Davis

AMACOM

American Management Association

New York • Atlanta • Brussels • Chicago • Mexico City • San Francisco
Shanghai • Tokyo • Toronto • Washington, D.C.

This publication is designed to provide accurate and authoritative information in regard
to the subject matter covered. It is sold with the understanding that the publisher is not
engaged in rendering legal, accounting, or other professional service. If legal advice or
other expert assistance is required, the services of a competent professional person should
be sought.

Library of Congress Cataloging-in-Publication Data

Davis, Kevin.
    Slow down, sell faster! : understand your customer's buying process and maximize
your sales / Kevin Davis.
        p.   cm.
    Includes bibliographical references and index.
    ISBN-13: 978-0-8144-1685-3
    Isbn-10: 0-8144-1685-3
    1. Consumer behavior.   2. Selling.   3. Customer relations.   I. Title.

    HF5415.32.D378   2011
    658.8'342—dc22

                                                          2010018024

Slow Down, Sell Faster! *is a trademark of TopLine Leadership, Inc.*

Slow Down, Sell Faster! *is a revised, rewritten, and updated edition of* Getting
Into Your Customer's Head *(Times Business © 1996).*

About AMA
American Management Association (www.amanet.org) is a world leader in talent
development, advancing the skills of individuals to drive business success. Our mission is
to support the goals of individuals and organizations through a complete range of
products and services, including classroom and virtual seminars, webcasts, webinars,
podcasts, conferences, corporate and government solutions, business books and
research. AMA's approach to improving performance combines experiential learning—
learning through doing—with opportunities for ongoing professional growth at every
step of one's career journey.

Printing number
10 9 8 7 6 5 4 3 2 1

To my parents, Bea and Clancy Davis,
for their love and guidance;
they always emphasized the importance
of rising to the challenge.

Contents

Foreword

S ales leaders are notoriously impatient. In sales meetings they talk about time-based competition. They quote from the book: "It's not the big that eat the small; it's the fast that eat the slow." They draw a sketch on the whiteboard explaining the current sales pipeline and asking everybody to accelerate sales. The battle cry in the sales office is "speed is your friend." Every sales leader wants fast sales; the trouble is, there aren't many fast buyers.

Unfortunately, speed often kills sales opportunities. I've seen too many salespeople chasing prospects at high speed until they realized they were chasing garbage trucks. If they had done their homework, they'd have learned to identify and go after the money trucks. Sometimes they are "chasing" so fast that they leave the truck in the dust, far behind.

Prospects take their time and they aren't going to speed up their process just because you are in a hurry. In *Slow Down, Sell Faster!*, Kevin Davis shows how you can speed up your sales—get more sales, faster—by *slowing down* your sales process. He provides a simple model that gives you clues about where your customer is in their buying process, and guidelines on what you can do to move the customer to the next step faster. The book has many memorable analogies that make it an easy and practical read for salespeople and their managers.

With all the talk about relationship-oriented selling, there have been very few books that spell out the "how to" of creating lasting relationships with customers. Kevin Davis shows the reader that every customer requires a different relationship style depending on what stage of buying he or she is in. The book offers a practical methodology that will give the reader a significant competitive advantage.

Someone once said that selling is like walking the road of agreement with your customer. If you are too fast, you'll lose the customer; if you are too slow, the customer will lose you. Selling at the right speed is an art. It's the art of reading your customers and staying in sync at all times with each customer's buying process. The right speed is best determined by the customer need. This book will teach you how to match speed and need.

Gerhard Gschwandtner
Founder and Publisher, *Selling Power*

Acknowledgments

M uch gratitude to our clients who, for the past twenty years, have entrusted us with the opportunity to work closely with their salespeople and sales managers. Many of the ideas and examples in this book grew out of the opportunities provided to us by our valued clients.

To Sue Reynard, freelance editor par excellence, and my close companion on this book journey for many months. On numerous occasions when I was at a loss for words Sue had the uncanny ability to tell me what I was thinking at the same time she was typing it. I'm very grateful for Sue's conversational and "tell-it-like-it-is" writing style.

Many thanks to Dennis Chopko, president of Killing Herb, Inc. and a very successful distributor of our sales training program. Dennis pored over this manuscript, then spent many hours on the phone with me providing detailed comments and constructive suggestions on every chapter. Dennis's tireless efforts have made this a much better book.

Many thanks also to Tom Cooke, president of Learning Outsource Group, a talented and successful distributor of *Getting Into Your Customer's Head* since 1998. Tom was an important catalyst for this book project, having badgered me (in a nice way) for the past five years to get started on this project.

Much appreciation to Tom Gundrum for his valuable contributions to TopLine Leadership, and our clients, since 1992.

Thank you to my good friend and European colleague Bill Zeeb, who was also instrumental in helping me to get started on this book project.

My gratitude also to those people who made this book a reality:

- ➤ To my agent Katie Kotchman at Don Congdon Associates, thanks for your unwavering belief and tireless efforts throughout these many months. Your impeccable integrity and thoughtful guidance is much appreciated.

- ➤ To Bob Nirkind, senior acquisitions editor at AMACOM Books, who read *Getting Into Your Customer's Head* and recognized the potential of *Slow Down, Sell Faster!* Bob provided numerous valuable suggestions and helped us to cross the finish line.

Over the years, the work of many authors has contributed to my understanding of selling and buying behavior. In addition to Professors Wind, Webster, and O'Shaughnessy (mentioned in the Introduction), Neil Rackham has been a thought leader in this area since the 1980s. Rackham's research-based approach to the understanding of buy-sell processes has made a significant contribution to the sales profession. I highly recommend Rackham's *SPIN Selling* (New York: McGraw-Hill, 1988) and *Major Account Sales Strategy* (New York: McGraw-Hill, 1989).

Thanks very much to the following people for submitting personal stories and anecdotes to *Slow Down, Sell Faster!*: Paul Auchincloss, Margaret Byrne, Patrick Coll, Jeannette Marshall, and James Rocha. Thanks also to Jessica Chen, Gary Connor, Ken Hartung, Chase Houston, Greg Kaiser, Scott Kranick, John Matovich, Corina Ojeda, Sandy Skiver, and John Sullivan.

Last but not least, thanks to my wife, Dale, for putting up with me for the past thirty years, and to our children Lauren and Kyle for continuing to ask, "How's the book coming, Dad?" over these many months.

Introduction

Years ago I was selling an office equipment solution to the CEO of a 100-person company. I was selling to him the way I had been taught: I established comfortable conversation while building trust, asked questions to diagnose his needs, then presented my solution as an answer to his needs. Everything appeared to be going along as planned. Suddenly he leaned forward and asked, "Aren't you going to *close* me now?"

Why is it that customers know more about selling techniques than most salespeople know about buying behavior? That's not right. **An understanding of buying is where selling should start.** We need to redefine "selling" to mean *helping people buy*.

What might "helping people buy" actually mean? The HR Chally Group, founded in 1973 through a grant from the United States Justice Department to create validated assessments that accurately predict on-the-job effectiveness—including sales performance, has a lot to say. For their most recent report Chally interviewed over 2,500 customers who provided opinions about more than 4,000 salespeople. The results appear in *The Chally World Class Sales Excellence Research Report*. Among their findings was that "customers usually award the prize to the salesperson who has been there through every step of their buying process, meeting customer need after customer need by presenting the right information at the right time. To win a sale, then, a salesperson's sales process must match perfectly with the customer's buying process. The two should be mirror images."[1]

We can take a lesson as well from Dr. Steven Covey's classic book, *7 Habits of Highly Effective People.* (I'd bet many of you have a copy on your bookshelf right now.) Dr. Covey says, "We have such a tendency to rush in, to fix things up with good advice. But we often fail to take the time to diagnose, to really, deeply understand the problem first."[2]

This rushing in and "fixing things up with good advice" occurs a lot in our profession because we have been conditioned to see things through a salesperson's eyes, and our sales behaviors are based on these perceptions. But your buyers have a different frame of reference. They have their own point of view.

So let me ask you, when selling, do you think as much about the customer's buying process as you do about your sales process? Are you with your customers "through every step of their buying process"?

If not, it's not your fault. Despite the evidence before us that a new sales paradigm is needed, few sales books or training courses teach salespeople how to deeply understand the purchasing decision from their customers' perspective, how to adapt their selling behavior to customers' buying behavior. If you don't think about the buying process on every call, you can get out of sync with your customer, and that can lead to lost sales.

That's why I wrote this book, to demonstrate the *why* and the *how* of getting in sync with your customer's buying process. When you do that, you realize that you need to slow down each conversation you have with a customer so you can ask more questions, and help the customer do a better job of buying. When you slow down your selling, you can help customers move more quickly through each step of their buying process. Hence the paradoxical title of this book: *Slow Down, Sell Faster!*

Helping Customers Buy

Most salespeople today believe they have evolved far beyond "traditional" selling. They think this is true because they define traditional selling as the "old-school" high-pressure, pushy, "press hard while signing here" sales approach. Salespeople see themselves as definitely *not* "traditional" because they have a more advanced sales process, no longer use controlling techniques, have better relationship-building skills, and truly care about the customer.

But stop for a moment to think about all the pressure that decision makers face today. The velocity of change is increasing; work of all types is interconnected via technology; there are different needs, constraints, and urgencies. They also face downsizing, reorganizations, and the fact that technological developments make today's decision makers more vulnerable to job loss. They may have the authority to buy, but not the permission to make a mistake. All these factors add up to customers experiencing more risk and uncertainty today, and require would-be purchasers to go through a deliberate buying process to avoid making a mistake.

That's why caring about your customer may get you in the door, but it can't guarantee you a sale because it doesn't help your customers do a better job of buying. What you need to do is link your sales strategy to customer buying behavior, a concept pioneered by former Dartmouth professor Frederick E. Webster, Jr. and University of Pennsylvania's Yoram Wind. Their 1972 publication *Organizational Buying Behavior* was decades ahead of its time and I highly recommend it for readers interested in the origin of advanced sales strategy.

Webster and Wind defined the steps of the customer buying process, and stated that organizational buying goes through predictable steps, that each decision maker has his/her own individual buying process, and that the buyer has more power than the seller—so you better focus on the customer.

They also identified what they called the Buying Center, a group of players with distinct roles in the purchasing decision, and discussed the impact of economic, technological, and political factors on those buying team members. They advise us to "determine at what stage in the decision process the prospect is working and lay plans for moving the organizational buyer from one stage to the next."[3] In short, forty years ago they were telling us to base our sales strategy on customer buying behavior. I've been following their advice for the past twenty years. (Wind and Webster haven't been given much credit and that's unfortunate.)

Webster and Wind's work is why I've come to define "traditional selling" as **any sales process not in sync with the psychology of buying.**

When it's put that way, would you now have to acknowledge that you are still using traditional selling? Could you say that you have truly joined your customer in their buying process? Wouldn't you like to have an alternative approach that *is* in sync with the psychology of buying? Doing so will help you make more sales because you will stay attuned to customers and choose the sales behavior that will more quickly move them through their buying process.

What You'll Find in This Book

The first chapter, in Part I of this book, introduces a selling model built around the customers' buying process. The model captures the essence of how selling must be redefined if you want to be in sync with your customers and build a competitive edge through the *way* you sell. Chapters 2 and 3 discuss the art of selling to multiple decision makers involved in a purchase, what I call a Complex Buying Team. Since most sales today involve more than one decision maker, these chapters describe what is now essential background information for almost every salesperson and provide the broader context for using the Sales Roles described in the main portion of this book.

Part II expands on the model introduced in Chapter 1. There are eight chapters named after the eight "roles"—student, doctor, architect, coach, therapist, negotiator, teacher, farmer—that match the steps of the customer's buying process. These professions are associated with the behaviors that will help you move your customer through their buying process (for instance, the "doctor" diagnoses symptoms, causes, and complications).

Each chapter starts with a brief introduction, then discusses what's happening with the customer during the buying step that is the focus of that chapter. The rest of the chapter talks about the matching sales role.

Part III includes just one chapter: a guide for sales managers on how to coach salespeople who are applying the sales model presented in this book.

Every chapter includes examples that will be useful to readers who are interested in developing more effective, buying-focused sales behaviors. When I'm in the market for a new book on selling the first thing I do is look for the author's examples of how to implement his or her ideas. I'm continually amazed at how many sales books tell me *what* to do but not *how* to do it. They have only a few (and often no) concrete examples. As a motivated salesperson striving to improve my selling skills, how am I supposed to apply a new sales technique if the author can't (or in some cases won't) show me how? If you have ever felt the same, then this book was written for you. No untested theories here. Just solid, proven strategies with lots of how-to examples.

What Has Changed Since the First Edition

Readers of the first edition of this book, *Getting Into Your Customer's Head*, may be wondering what is new and different about this book. The one thing that *hasn't* changed is the sales model. No sense reinventing the wheel. Apart from that, every chapter has been rewritten with lots of new ideas. In addition:

- Because selling today is much more complex than in 1996, what in my first book was the *final* chapter, "Winning the Complex Sale," has been significantly expanded and now appears in two chapters at the beginning of the book (Chapter 2: Mastering the Politics of Selling to Multiple Decision Makers and Chapter 3: Strategies for Winning the Complex Sale).
- I broke out four outcome-based Milestones that punctuate the selling process and provide built-in opportunities for formulating your sales strategy.
- When I wrote *Getting Into Your Customer's Head* I had fifteen years of sales, sales management, and sales training experience. Now I have thirty years. I hope it shows.
- Old stories have been replaced with recent client examples.

> Useful tips have been added throughout.
> I added a new chapter for sales managers that provides advice on how to improve the effectiveness of their coaching skills in general and shows them what to look for as they help their salespeople through each step of the sales process.

Why Should You Listen to Me?

My sales career began thirty years ago selling office equipment for Lanier, something like the "Marine Corps" of business-to-business sales. I'd take the elevator to the top floor of an office building and cold call my way down to the lobby. I was taught to walk into an office and ask to see the General Manager for "just ten minutes." With good technique and twenty cold calls per day, I could see three prospects. Then in the afternoon I'd call the seventeen prospects I didn't get in to see that morning, seeking an appointment. After a few years on the street I moved up to major accounts, where our "system sale" to hospitals could run $500k and up, a complex sale to multiple levels of decision makers. I then became a sales manager, and eventually a general manager, during which time I hired, trained, and coached over 200 salespeople.

One day in April 1989 I was out working in the field with one of my salespeople. I stopped into a bookstore in La Jolla, California, looking for a book that might offer me new ideas for improving the quality of my next sales meeting. That's when I saw it: *Why People Buy* by John O'Shaughnessy, Professor of Business at the Columbia University School of Business.[4] Professor O'Shaughnessy and his research assistants interviewed both businesses and consumers about their buying decisions. The researchers found that when buyers feel uncertain about which product or service to buy (and who doesn't?) they will seek to resolve their uncertainty with a rational and predictable buying process. For me, it was a blinding flash of the obvious! My entire sales career had been spent thinking about *sales techniques* rather than *buying behavior*.

Three months later, I resigned from Lanier and hung out my shingle as a sales trainer. Operating in start-up mode out of a spare bedroom in a small suburb of San Diego, I knew I had found the right calling. Six years later, in 1996, my first book, *Getting Into Your Customer's Head,* was published.

Since 1989 my company, along with our valued and talented distributor partners in the United States and Canada, have implemented the *Getting Into Your Customer's Head* sales approach in many successful corporate sales organizations, from dozens of major multinational corporations to hundreds of small and medium-sized firms. Our clients have come from many different sectors: software, document management, transportation, business services, career/staffing services, financial services, professional services, wireless, telecom, healthcare, heavy equipment, media . . . you name it.

Who This Book Is For

This book focuses on sales situations where customers go through a deliberate decision-making process before making a purchase, and often there is more than one person involved in the decision. These are the situations where the need is greatest for a salesperson to develop a deep understanding of the customer's thoughts and emotions about the purchase, and to get their *sales* process in line with the customer's *buying* process.

Those who will find the book most useful are business-to-business salespeople (both outside and inside) whose products or services are considered "major" purchases by their customers, and business-to-consumer salespeople who offer high-dollar products or services, particularly if there is more than one decision maker involved. Using the techniques described in this book will help you learn more about your customers' decision-making process and therefore sell to them more effectively.

Win-Win Selling

Habit 4 in Steven Covey's book is *Think Win/Win*. Covey says, "You can only achieve Win/Win solutions with Win/Win processes—the end and the means are the same."[5]

I agree! If you want to sell win-win solutions, you must have a win-win sales process. This is not optional. And it means something has to change. Customers don't care about the steps of your sale, they care about getting their needs met. They are unlikely to change their buying process to match your selling process, so your only option is to be the one who switches.

I challenge you to **slow down**, to make buying-focused selling your core sales approach. Prospects and customers are waiting.

PART I

Understanding Buying Is Where Selling Should Start

CHAPTER 1

Why Slower Is Faster

How Selling Too Fast Results in Lost Sales and a Longer Buying Process

R ecently I was retained by a regional VP of sales for a large financial institution to evaluate the effectiveness of his team's sale of investment advisory services provided to high-net-worth customers. He asked me to be a "mystery shopper," and at his request I met with one of his salespeople while posing as a high-net-worth customer considering the possibility of changing from my current financial advisor to another investment management firm.

Coincidentally, at the time I actually had a few concerns about my own personal financial advisor, and because I realized that I might change firms as a result of my analysis, I told my client that in order to perform a realistic decision process, I would also meet with two of his company's competitors. (It's also why I asked to meet his best and most experienced advisor, figuring that's who I'd want working for me should I decide to actually pick this firm.)

Over the next six weeks I met as planned with the representatives of three different investment advisory firms, including one from my client's firm. Each of the sales consultants was extremely effective at building rapport, making me feel comfortable, and creating a perception of caring.

Yet they all made the single most common mistake that salespeople in all industries make: they moved through the steps of their sales process—building trust, identifying needs, presenting their solutions, going for the close—without thinking about where I was in my decision-making process. **They sold too fast.** They put me on *their* sales track, instead of joining me in *my* buying process.

That's why this book has the paradoxical title of *Slow Down, Sell Faster!* When you sell slower on each sales call—ask more questions and do many of the activities suggested in this book—your customers will buy faster. They will more fully recognize their needs and the urgency of those needs. The best solution (hopefully yours) will be more clearly defined and differentiated in ways the customer recognizes as important. It is this connection with the customer's buying process that will differentiate you.

In this chapter, I want to talk in more detail about what I mean by saying these financial advisors sold too fast, discuss how customers buy, and present a new model of selling that matches the customer buying process.

How Selling Too Fast Causes Lost Sales

My first face-to-face meeting with my client's investment advisor went as follows (the labels are mine, the actions were the advisor's):

- **Build trust:** The advisor began by learning a bit about me, before sharing about himself, his money management background, education, etc. It was an effective opening.
- **Identify needs:** The advisor then asked me some questions. He learned about my financial goals, and that I was dissatisfied with the returns and performance achieved by my current financial advisor.
- **Present solution overview:** He explained that his firm's approach is not to be market timers or "fad chasers," and he

told me about his firm's investment model that minimizes risk while maximizing returns. I also learned that his approach to determining his clients' needs was to create a Personal Wealth Plan based on my answers to questions such as: Where is my money now? Where would my financial assets be in retirement?

> **Close for next step:** The advisor then recommended we meet again in a few days, and asked that I bring account statements of my current investments.

Here are the five mistakes he made—all of which revolve around selling too fast:

1. He didn't delve into *why* I thought my returns with my current advisor were poor. If he had, I would have explained that over the previous eight years my portfolio hadn't really changed all that much—that there had been little movement of assets from one investment type to another. My opinion was that my current advisor was lazy and took my account for granted. **Had my client's advisor asked the right questions, he would have gained deeper insight into my needs, and he would have been much more persuasive later during his solution presentation.**

2. Since he didn't know about my current advisor's laziness and slow response, he forfeited one of the most powerful tools a salesperson has: **getting prospects to think about the possible negative consequences of *not* making a change.** In this case, had he asked about what would happen if I did nothing, I would have thought about the effect of trusting my money to someone asleep at the switch, and about all the fear and uncertainty that that would have entailed. That would have helped me put a face on my future.

3. He didn't try to find out about my second need. Usually, the first topic discussed with a prospective client is his or her greatest concern at that time; it's the need that's most developed from the customer's perspective, and the reason the customer agreed to meet with you. **Getting prospects to realize they have more than one need for change creates a**

Tip: Probing for the Second Need

During a first meeting with a customer, it's unlikely they will tell you everything going on in their decision process. For all you know, the first need they mention may be something identified by one of your competitors in a meeting the day before! By failing to probe for the second need, you may be allowing your competitor to define your customer's mental picture of a solution. Not good.

Even if your customer hasn't talked with your competitors, probing for a second need is a good way to get him or her to increase their desire for change. In my meeting with the financial advisor, he should have asked, "Other than lackluster investment returns, is there anything else about your current advisor that concerns you?" In doing so, he would have learned that I felt my monthly statements were too complex. My entire portfolio was not available for me to see on a single web page. So I was in the dark about important concerns such as the overall asset allocation of my investments. Had his company been able to provide that service, I would have seen more advantages to making a change.

greater sense of urgency, which adds greater potential value to the solution you will eventually offer (see sidebar).

4. He didn't ask me about my buying process—how I would make my decision regarding who would get my business. So he didn't learn that I was going to be interviewing two of his competitors. **He lost out on an opportunity to start answering my question "why should I choose you" before I asked it of him.**

5. He didn't ask me who else would be involved in my decision. While I could have been acting alone, had the advisor asked he would have learned that my wife is a valued partner in our financial decisions. **He could have then sped up our buying decision by slowing down his sales pitch and requesting a follow-up meeting with both me and my wife.** (In fact, most sales situations today involve more than one decision maker. Gaining access to the second or third or fourth decision maker is therefore key, and is something I'll cover in Chapters 3 and 5).

When I met with the advisor the following day, he continued to make even more mistakes, maintaining his focus on his selling process rather than on my buying process. (In case you're curious, I did eventually hire one of the three advisors I interviewed, and am very happy with my choice.)

In a way, I wasn't surprised by this advisor's behavior. His company had put their salespeople through a lot of traditional sales training. Also, I've observed that more-experienced salespeople are the most likely to sell too fast. Why? One reason is that the "expert" salesperson has seen the customer's problem before, and assumes that the customer now sees it, too. As a result, he or she jumps immediately into describing their product's or service's benefits before the customer has fully recognized the scope of the problem. (New salespeople lack application expertise, so they're more likely to ask additional questions that get the customer talking about needs and applications.)

No matter whether you're just selling as you've been taught to sell, or showing off your knowledge of the subject to your prospect, jumping ahead of the customer means you are pitching too much information too soon. This only serves to dampen the customer's curiosity. (Have you ever noticed that customers are easy to reach when they need your information, but almost impossible to reach when they don't?) You play the customer. Suppose I present you with ten capabilities of my product or service, but you think you only need five of them. How will it make you feel? The natural reaction is either that "this is more than I need/it's too expensive," or "maybe somebody else has a better solution for my company's needs."

Every salesperson wants to sell more. We all want to make more money and gain recognition for peak performance. As my experience with the financial advisor illustrates, the way to do this is to **slow down.** We need to take the time to get into our customer's head, because that's how we can learn more about their needs, and how their focus and concerns change as they move through their buying process. With a better understanding of a customer's needs and concerns, we provide more value throughout their buying process. We can help them become clearer about the opportunity and risks they face; help them better define criteria for an ideal solution. When these issues are clearly spelled out, customers become more comfortable with their decision. They can reach their purchasing decision more quickly. And that's how you **sell faster**.

Shifting from Selling- to Buying-Focused

Over the past twenty years as a sales consultant, I've delivered hundreds of sales seminars. I start by asking salespeople two questions. The first question is, "What are the steps of your selling process?" Here, I get clear, concise answers. Most salespeople can describe how they sell. One answer I hear often is "Open, Needs, Support, and Close." Another is "Prepare, Qualify, Present, Objections, and Close." While the answers vary from one salesperson to another, and from one company to another, the point is clear: Most salespeople have a well-thought-out and well-defined sales process that they follow.

The second question is, "What are the steps of your customer's buying process?" Even today, with an increased emphasis on being customer-focused, that question still stumps people. Some have never thought about the process from the customer's viewpoint, and even those who are trying to be more customer-driven haven't formalized their thinking to the point where they can appreciate the process that customers go through when making major purchases. The result is that salespeople tend to think about what they're doing during the sales process to try to sell, rather than what the customer needs to do to make an educated buying decision.

One of the first lessons I try to pass on to salespeople is that *customers don't care about your sales process*. They care about their buying process.

The Eight Steps in the Customer's Buying Process

People and organizations buy in two ways:

1. *Buy-knowing:* When buyers already know as much as they need to know in order to buy, they quickly make a decision.

2. *Buy-learning:* When buyers do *not* have all the information they need to make an educated purchasing decision, they need to do some research and learn more first.

Because the customers who are operating in a buy-*knowing* mode are likely to make up their minds without dealing with a salesperson, the customers we will focus on in this book are those operating in a buy-*learning* mode. They are going through a more deliberate, predictable process.

The major premise of this book is that understanding the customer's buying process and adapting your sales behavior accordingly is what will give you a competitive edge.

Because the steps of buying are a process, I created a model that shows them as a wheel (see Figure 1-1). This wheel captures the four phases of buying that customers in a buy-learning mode typically go through:

1. Identifying a *need*
2. *Learning* more about their options
3. *Buying* the good or service
4. Evaluating the *value* of that purchase

Need . . . Learn . . . Buy . . . Value . . . those are the customer's purposes, the end game of each phase of buying. But dig a little deeper,

Figure 1-1 The Four Stages of Buying

Figure 1-2 The Eight Steps of Customer Buying

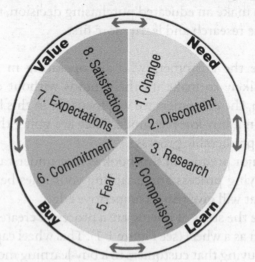

and you'll see that customers go through eight steps—two distinct steps in each phase—as shown in Figure 1-2.

For example, think about the last time you were in a buy-learning mode, making a big purchase such as buying a car or a house. Everything started with a *Change* in your life (Step 1). Did you have children? Move to different area of the country with different weather conditions? That change triggered *Discontent* with your current situation (Step 2). Discontent can be caused by a problem (such as a wrecked car) or an opportunity being missed (such as a new job that pays you more money and causes you to feel dissatisfied with your old clunker).

Once your discontent has developed into a need you decided to learn about the options you had. First, you did *Research* (Step 3) to identify alternative solutions (houses in different neighborhoods, different models of cars or minivans), then did a *Comparison* (Step 4) of potential solutions (different car models or different houses).

Eventually you identified a preferred solution and were about to buy. But if you're like most of us, there was a moment of *Fear,* when you weren't sure you were doing the right thing or making the right choice (Step 5). You walked out of the showroom or told your realtor you wanted to "think it over." You may not have returned the salesperson's calls until you had rethought the decision. Eventually, I'm assuming, you worked through your fears and made a *Commitment* to the purchase (Step 6).

For many salespeople—the car salesperson or realtor in our scenario—that's where the sales process would end because the purchase has been made. But from *your* point of view as the customer, the important part of the buying process is just beginning, you want to see if the value you receive meets your *Expectations* (Step 7). If yes, you ultimately reach a state of *Satisfaction* with the purchase (Step 8) . . . until, that is, something changes and you go through the cycle again.

Six Mysteries of Selling Solved

If you follow a sales process that does not match the steps of the customer buying process, you end up making inadvertent mistakes. When you become more familiar with what is going on in the customer's head at each step of their buying process, you will be able to explain some of the most common mysteries of selling, including:

> **Why so many of your telephone prospecting calls fall on deaf ears.** Most salespeople include in their approach call a "benefit statement," which is two or three generic customer benefits that attempt to create interest so the prospect agrees to an initial appointment. But the vast majority of prospects are either in the *Change* or *Discontent* steps when you call them. They may or may not be aware they have a problem, which means they are nowhere near having the kind of explicit need for a solution that would allow them to respond positively to your pitch. Describing benefits is a match for a customer's state of mind much later in the buying process, in the *Comparison* step. In talking about benefits off the bat, you're out of sync, steps ahead of your customer—and, unfortunately for you, buyers rarely skip steps.

▷ **Why customers ask you early on to give them a "ballpark" price.** In the *Need* phase, buyers are trying to determine whether the discomfort they are feeling is a serious enough issue to warrant attention. They are wondering, "Is this a big enough priority that we should explore purchasing a solution?" By asking you to give a ballpark estimate of the cost, they are looking for data that will enable them to compare cost versus benefit, and judge whether it's worth going any further with their purchasing decision. If the price seems reasonable compared to the seriousness of the problem, they are more likely to continue along the buying process. If it is expensive relative to the perceived impact, they may bring the process to a halt.

▷ **Why customers fail to recognize the full value of your solution and resort to pushing back on price.** As salespeople, most of us have been trained to present our solution as soon as we have identified the customer's needs. Trouble is, that usually occurs when the customer is in either the *Discontent* or *Research* steps. That means we are discussing our features and options when the customer still only has a vague notion at best regarding the urgency of the need, let alone what an ideal solution would look like. Until they fully understand their needs—including *the consequences of inaction*—and they have a vivid mental picture of a solution, they are not in a position to appreciate the value of what you're offering.

▷ **Why nothing happens after an initial meeting that seemingly went great.** Following an initial meeting, the person you met with typically reaches out to another decision maker and, you hope, effectively sells the other person on why their organization should further examine this issue. Yet few salespeople provide their prospects with sales tools (matched to where they are in the buying process) that they can use to persuade other decision makers that a need may exist. A sales brochure is not the answer here. You need to provide more persuasive tools for your prospect to sell others on your behalf.

> **Why customers go silent at the eleventh hour.** It's happened to every salesperson I know: they develop a good relationship with the client, focus on needs, develop a proposal, deliver a strong presentation, get positive signals from their supporters within the account . . . and then, just when they think the sale will go through, they suddenly can't get the prospect to return their phone call. This happens because it's rare for a buyer to go directly from comparing options to committing to one solution. Customers "go silent" because they are in the *Fear* step, experiencing doubts and concerns about everything from making the purchase at all to what others may think of their choice. When you learn to anticipate fear and maintain communication, you can take action to prevent it from derailing your sale.

> **How competitors sneak in the back door.** When salespeople present their product or service during the customer's *Research* step, they arrive at what they consider "the close" at the precise point the customer begins his or her *Comparison* step by talking to other potential suppliers (the competition). The salesperson's sales process concludes and communication with the customer is lost, just when their competitors' sales process is beginning. Not good.

How Buying Impacts Selling

I have a book published by *Harvard Business Review* titled *Business Classics: Fifteen Key Concepts for Managerial Success*.[6] The book contains the fifteen articles in *HBR*'s history that have sold the most reprints. One article, "What Makes a Good Salesman" by David Mayer and Herbert Greenberg, was published in 1964. The authors' research found that there are two qualities that make an effective salesperson: *ego-drive* (or personal ambition) and *empathy*. For my purposes, empathy is the more important of the two; it reflects your capacity to experience something through the eyes of another (in this case, your customer).

And yet, five decades after that article was published, salespeople are seldom selected for a sales job because they are empathetic, nor are they taught empathy after being hired. The predominance of sales training literature is still focused on the steps of the sale, the things that salespeople need to do to sell the customer: prospect, approach, question, qualify, present, handle objections, close, etc. Are we still in the 1960s, or what?

A central theme of this book is that once you appreciate a purchase from the customer's perspective, you stop thinking of selling as a *sales process*, and start thinking of it as *facilitating the customer's buying process*.

In short, buying is where selling should start. The customer buying process should be your starting point; then you match your sales approach to the customer's buying behavior. When you do this you achieve more sales and greater customer satisfaction.

The Eight Sales Roles That Match the Buying Process

You want to sell more, and you want to sell faster. Here are the necessary ingredients:

1. Define the steps your customer goes through when making a buying decision.

2. Match the steps of your sale to your customer's decision-making process.

3. Plan every sales call by asking yourself, "Where is this prospect at in his/her decision-making process?" and "What does this customer need to learn in order to take the next step?"

We've just been through the steps a customer in a buy-learning mode typically goes through (ingredient #1). The question for you, therefore, is "How can I help a customer get through those steps

Figure 1-3 The Sales Wheel

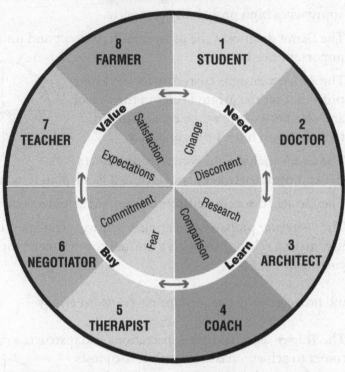

This wheel shows the eight sales roles a sales consultant needs to use to match a customer's buying steps.

faster (and, frankly, in a way that shifts the odds in my favor)?" The answer is that you have to recognize that the kind of support a customer needs varies by what step of the process they are in, so you must shift the role you play to provide that exact kind of support.

Taking the customer's buying process as the core, in Figure 1-3 I've mapped out the eight sales roles most suited to helping your customers through their buying steps.

As shown on the wheel, the model includes *six roles where you are acting as a sales consultant* for the customer's buying process . . .

1. The *Student* studies the change affecting the customer and approaches high probability prospects.

2. The *Doctor* diagnoses the prospect's discontent and uncovers important needs.

3. The *Architect* designs customer-focused solutions that set the ground rules in their favor, and clarifies exactly which capabilities in their solution must be highlighted.

4. The *Coach* analyzes the competition, selects the appropriate strategy, and creates a game plan to win.

5. The *Therapist* draws out customer fears and helps to resolve them.

6. The *Negotiator* prepares and applies win-win strategies to not just make a sale but to reach a mutual commitment with the customer.

. . . and *two roles where you are cultivating customer loyalty*:

7. The *Teacher* sets customer expectations and instructs a customer to achieve maximum value, then tests to make sure that the value promised the customer has in fact been achieved.

8. The *Farmer* nourishes customer satisfaction in order to grow the relationship.

I've used the names of common professions for each of these roles because they capture the essential theme of the behaviors needed to help a customer. (The "architect," for example, is designing a solution for a customer who is researching his or her options.) I've found these labels help make the model easy to use and apply. The result is that, at each step of the buying process, you will meet your customers' needs better than your competitors do. That's a competitive advantage!

The Need–Learn–Buy–Value ring that connects the salesperson to the customer is an important part of this graphic as well. To determine needs, the customer goes through *Change* and *Discontent*.

The salesperson is also committed to determining the customer's needs, which is why they adopt the Student and Doctor roles. In the Learn stage, the customer has to learn and so does the salesperson. In the Buy stage, salespeople need to help customers resolve their buying fears so they will be comfortable making a commitment to buy. The customer's ultimate goal is achieving Value, and salespeople must strive to help them achieve it to create loyal customers who will do repeat business with their company.

The bi-directional arrows are also significant. While we all hope the customer's buying process moves forward, there are times when it is in a customer's best interest for you to get them to move backwards. For example, if your professional opinion is that your customer has misdiagnosed their own needs, following through on your customer-focused responsibility requires that you at least try to get that customer to move backwards and reexamine their needs. (And, as we know all too well, customers often move backwards in their buying process without any help from salespeople.)

As the sales wheel graphic points out, the entire sales process is about creating customer loyalty. But lasting loyalty is not achieved until, first, customer satisfaction is achieved. Without satisfaction

---

Tip: How to Use the Sales Wheel

No doubt you've heard the saying, "a picture is worth a thousand words." The sales wheel is a picture of sales effectiveness, a memory aid to help you utilize and apply more of what you read. Later chapters of this book will explore each of these roles, describing in more detail what the customer is going through and how the matched sales role can help you achieve your sales goal: getting customers through each step faster, with the odds shifted in your favor.

Salespeople have told me that having a simple graphic, a model, that integrates both buying behavior and selling behavior makes it easier for them to get in sync with their customers and make more sales. Some keep the graphic on their desk or carry it with them as a daily reminder to slow down and not slip back into old selling habits.

there can be no loyalty. It is only by completing the full process with the customer—not abandoning them after you've completed the sale—that you can create the kind of satisfaction that can lead to long-term loyalty.

Using the Roles to Engage in the Customer's Buying Process

Having a strong plan every time you make contact with a customer is what this book is all about. I want you to be able to book more appointments with senior executives and learn how to ask more effective questions that create a greater demand to buy; I want you to be able to outsell your competitors by setting the ground rules in your favor before your competition gets in the door.

And if your competition does get in the door, as they usually do, you'll be equipped with new competitive sales strategies that get your customer to push your competitors back outside.

You'll also learn the secrets of negotiating the big sale, and how to bring home a complex sale with multiple decision makers.

You'll learn how to get into your customer's head. You'll learn how to become a partner in your customer's buying process, helping them move forward step by step, by:

1. Identifying a compelling reason or benefit for the customer to change.
2. Influencing the customer's application—how they will use your product or service—so that they see your solution as the clear and compelling best choice. To do this you must connect your solution's differentiators with the customer's explicit needs.
3. Gaining access to the multiple decision makers and helping them see both the compelling reason for change and the superiority of your solution.
4. Presenting a winning proposal that effectively communicates your value in the customer's terms, tailored to the different concerns of each of the decision makers.
5. Spelling out exactly what you will do to ensure a successful implementation.

6. Measuring the results you deliver or, even better, have your customer measure the results of your solution.

7. Communicating those results with senior executives within the customer's business and growing the relationship. (In my view, you don't really have a customer until they buy from you a second time.)

Slow Down and Get in Sync!

You may think you're doing a good job of selling because you've abandoned the high-pressure sales tactics of the past. You reject the "self-focused product pusher with commission breath" approach. You genuinely care about your customers.

But what really matters is not how you perceive yourself, but how your customers perceive you. And I guarantee you this: Salespeople who continue to move ahead in their sales process and ignore where the customer is in their buying process are going to be perceived by customers as selfish, more concerned about themselves than the customer.

I have one mission in this book: **to convince you to slow down your sales process and get in sync with your customer.** I want you to become a fascinated observer of your customers' buying processes and not assume that the buying will occur the same way each time.

By slowing down and looking at a purchase from the customer's *buying* perspective, you will become sensitive to the twists and turns that would have sent you off track in the past. You will gain a better understanding of customer problems—certainly better than your competitors' and likely better than customers have themselves. Your insights will better prepare you to resolve the challenges both you and your customer face at each step along the way. That's how you can help your customers move more quickly through their buying process. And that's why if you slow down, you sell faster!

CHAPTER 2

Mastering the Politics of Selling to Multiple Decision Makers

It's happened to all of us. We put in a lot of time and effort into a sale, and then at the eleventh hour that sweet sure thing disintegrates. Often the cause of these failures is a lack of mastery over the politics of the complex sale (one involving multiple decision makers). I once completed a successful sale, and delivered a well-received training workshop to the client's major account salespeople. Though the workshop got excellent reviews, an anticipated (and much larger) second sale to the same client fell through. Why? There was an executive who had ruffled feathers because he hadn't been involved in the decision to hire my company.

In my business, and I suspect in yours as well, the simple sale involving only one decision maker is getting rarer and rarer. There will likely be multiple decision makers, each with different interests, needs, and degrees of influence—and each likely to be at a different step of the buying process at any given point in time. Mastering the politics of the complex sale and developing strategies for dealing with multiple players at different buying steps is critical to being a successful salesperson.

In this chapter, I'll quickly review the players involved in a complex decision, then describe how the decision-making process typically unfolds when multiple players are involved, and provide a case study to illustrate the key points. In the next chapter, I'll discuss what to do with this knowledge to win a complex sale. (If you only sell to one decision maker, you may want to skip directly to Part II.)

The Players on a Complex Buying Team

Perhaps not surprisingly, the composition of a Complex Buying Team can itself be complex. Each player will be a unique combination of four characteristics, involving whether they have the authority to make the final call, what aspects of the solution they are interested in, whether they wield special influence or power on the team, and ultimately whether they decide to support you or work against you.

These characteristics mean that there are four lenses for analyzing the composition of a Complex Buying Team. Figure 2-1 summarizes the lenses and the types of labels given to the player positions in each category. The next sections go through each characteristic and describe the labels and how they are used.

Figure 2-1 Four Lenses for Analyzing Team Composition

1 Final call	2 Interests	3 Information & Access Control	4 Support
ROI Authority*	ROI Authority	Power Broker**	Sponsor***
	User/ Super User	Gatekeeper*	Anti-Sponsor***
	Integrator		

* Only one per team.
** Often one per group or department
*** Sponsors and Anti-Sponsors are created based on what happens in the buying process. Other players exist automatically.

Tip: ROI Authorities May Be in the Background

An important aspect of working with ROI Authorities is recognizing that they are usually visible only at the beginning of the buying process, again when the choice is being made, and then well after implementation to determine the return on investment. (Chapter 3 has more details on why this happens and what to do about it.) If you initiated the sales opportunity, you may be able to gain access to this person up front. But if the customer called you, then it's likely they have passed the needs-identification stage of the buying process, and it's likely the ROI Authority will operate mostly in the background until much later in the process.

Lens 1: Who Makes the Final Call?

The single person (or in some cases the single entity, such as a board of directors) who makes the final decision is called the ROI Authority. (The ROI part is explained in Lens 2.) This is the person who can say yes or no. It is *the person whose budget is at stake.*

Lens 2: Who Is Interested in What?

Every person inside your prospective client who is involved in the buying decision is basically interested in one (or more) of three types of issues, as shown in Figure 2-2.

Figure 2-2 Driving Interests of Buying Team Members

Player	What They Pay Attention To
ROI Authority	Return on investment Priority of this opportunity compared to others
User and Super User	Functionality; ease of use
Integrator	Compatibility with existing systems/technology

> **ROI Authority:** This person will be *interested primarily in the bottom line,* that is, the return on investment or payback

period. However, early on his or her goal is to make sure the problem is defined clearly and correctly. Note as well that this individual usually has a broad scope of responsibility and therefore might be comparing the investment required for solving the problem that your solution addresses to other entirely different types of investments. From the ROI Authority's perspective, it's a matter of priorities.

- **User or Super User:** As the name implies, a User is a person who will use your product/service. A Super User is either someone nominated to represent other Users or is the manager (or supervisor) of the people who will use it. These are individuals who live every day with the problem you're trying to solve, and therefore have the best understanding of operational issues. They are *primarily interested in the functionality of your solution and how it will affect their jobs.* Users can endorse options, but not make the final choice. They also can often eliminate a potential supplier from the running ("I don't think we can work with them . . ." or "This solution looks too complicated").

- **Integrator:** This label refers to anyone with expert knowledge who will *evaluate both technical issues* (the performance criteria your product/service must meet) *and compatibility issues* (how your product or service integrates with others already in service). As with Users, an Integrator's opinion can be used to eliminate a potential supplier from consideration; their approval is usually a prerequisite for making the final cut.

In addition, the jobs of the different players will affect the focus of their attention. Suppose, for example, you were selling a component for an automobile. The Complex Buying Teams you'd encounter would include engineers (possibly in consultation with R&D) who would be looking at particular performance characteristics; production managers, who would be concerned about maintaining smooth production operations and minimizing quality problems (and therefore reluctant to change equipment and procedures, should your new product require them); the purchasing department, whose bias would likely be to stick with the company's current vendors (provided the price is acceptable); the legal department, who would be looking at any potential liabilities your new product might introduce; and a CFO or other executive who wants to control costs. If this were your sales opportunity, you would have to address all of these concerns at different points in the customer's buying process.

Lens 3: Information and Access Control

Getting access to all players on a complex buying team is critical if you want to succeed. There are two types of people who can either greatly help or hinder you in that quest: Power Brokers and Gatekeepers.

The most important player on a complex buying team is the **Power Broker**, the individual on the team with the greatest influence and the political clout for swaying other buyers. This is the person on the team who has the greatest credibility at the executive level (including the ROI Authority)—and, in fact, the Power Broker may actually be the ROI Authority, but more often is a User, Super User, Gatekeeper, or Integrator. Because their credibility is on the line, they will be looking at overall business effectiveness, not just the specific characteristics typically associated with their other responsibility. They will also have to explain the return on investment to the ROI Authority.

Sometimes the Power Broker is a person officially designated by the ROI Authority to take the validated need and explore the solution options; other times, he or she is just someone with a lot of personal credibility within the client organization. But whether the power is formal or informal, the Power Broker plays a crucial role in the flow of information and access. He or she will assimilate information gathered by the team and make a recommendation to the ROI Authority (see Figure 2-3).

Power Brokers come in different shapes and sizes. Some will exert influence by seeking to reach a consensus among different decision makers; others simply try to exert influence with the ROI Authority and basically say it's "my way or the highway." This latter

Figure 2-3 The Power Broker's Influence

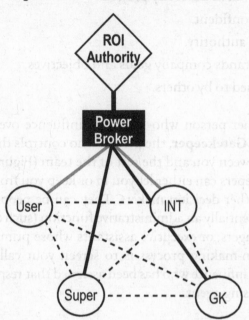

type of Power Broker says, "To heck with the conflict, this needs to happen." Or, "Damn the torpedoes, full speed ahead." In so doing, the involvement and opinions of other decision makers are discounted, which can easily create animosity going forward.

Power Brokers who are consensus builders have a high need to accommodate others and want to follow existing rules; they tend to be people-oriented, outgoing, and optimistic. They use expressive gestures and are concerned about what others think. Damn-the-torpedoes types tend to be task-oriented, strong, and forceful.

To have a winning sales strategy, you must identify and then influence the Power Broker. It can be difficult to identify this trusted adviser: job titles are not reliable clues. If not formally designated, listen to what other team members say and to whom *they* listen (the informal leader on a Complex Buying Team). In general, the Power Broker will be the person who:

➢ Has access to senior managers.

➢ Has the most to gain—or lose—politically from a buying decision.

> Is involved in other key projects.
> Is self-confident.
> Desires authority.
> Understands company goals and objectives.
> Is listened to by others.

The other person who has a big influence over access to the team is the **Gatekeeper**, the person who controls the flow of information between you and the rest of the team (Figure 2-4).

Gatekeepers can either let you in or keep you from making contact with other decision makers. They can be people who are performing essentially an administrative function (such as receptionists, office managers, or executive assistants whose primary function in the decision-making process is to screen your call) or a decision maker with influence who has been assigned that responsibility, such as a purchasing agent.

Lens 4: Do They Support You or Are They Against You?

Ultimately, each decision maker on a team will either be for you or against you. You can categorize the roles as:

> **Sponsor:** Any decision maker who wants your solution to succeed.

> **Anti-Sponsor:** Any decision maker who does not want their company to purchase from you. They could be opposed to

Figure 2-4 The Gatekeeper's Role

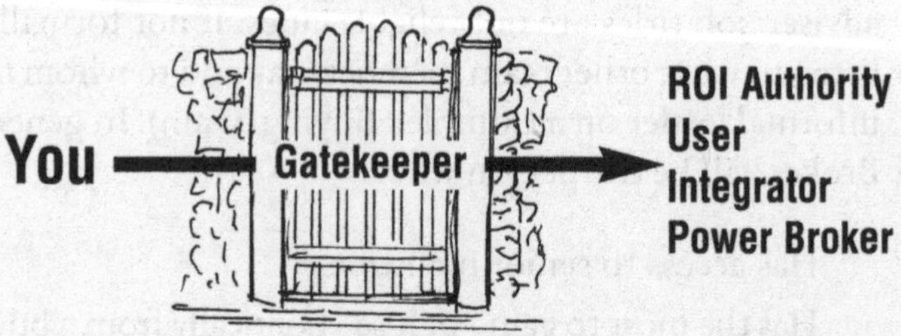

You ——→ Gatekeeper ——→ ROI Authority
User
Integrator
Power Broker

you for any number of reasons: perhaps they have strong ties to another solution provider, don't think the investment is needed at all, or are having an internal power struggle with your Sponsors! The Anti-Sponsor is the greatest threat to your winning a complex sale. They often operate in stealth and may not want you to know that they are against your solution. (More on this later.)

The key to winning a complex sale is selling to as many members of the Complex Buying Team as you can reach and turning as many as possible into Sponsors. (See Figure 2-5.)

Figure 2.5 Sponsors or Anti-Sponsors?

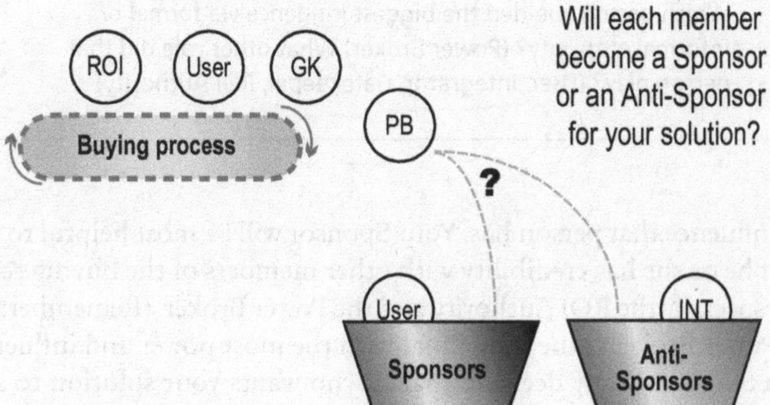

Since the Power Broker has the most influence on the team, naturally you want to try to develop a strong relationship with that person and hopefully turn him or her into a Sponsor. Doing so will give you access to inside information as you are diagnosing needs and helping the client shape a mental image of an ideal solution; it will also give you a lot of what I call "relationship power" when it comes to negotiating (see Chapter 9).

How to Cultivate Sponsors

A Sponsor is someone who wants you to succeed, who wants your solution to win. But you need to be aware of how much power and

---

Tip: Think About How Decisions Are Made in *Your* Company

It can be difficult figuring out which people are playing which decision-making roles. What I've found helps is to start by thinking of a recent major decision made inside your own company.

▷ Who made the final call and determined what budget would be affected? (ROI Authority)

▷ Which people are directly affected by the decision and have to implement the change? (Users)

▷ Who was concerned about trying to make sure the outcome of the decision would fit seamlessly into current operations? (Integrator)

▷ Which person wielded the biggest influence via formal or informal authority? (Power Broker) What other role did that person play? (User, Integrator, Gatekeeper, ROI Authority)

---

influence that person has. Your Sponsor will be most helpful to you if he or she has credibility with other members of the buying team, especially the ROI Authority and the Power Broker. (Remember: the Power Broker is the individual with the most power and influence; a Sponsor is any decision maker who wants your solution to succeed.) Without credibility with others, the sales effectiveness of your Sponsor is greatly diminished, and any access to inside information is limited.

Because you need at least one Sponsor to win a major sale (more are better), it makes sense to develop one as early as possible in the buying process. If you can identify and gain access to the Power Broker before your competitors do and help him or her become a "Power Sponsor," your sale is *almost* assured.

The best Sponsor is the person with the strongest *personal* benefit associated with your unique solution. Although business buyers have an interest in achieving their organization's goals, their motivation in the buying process is usually derived from both their personal and business goals.

For example, Kurt, a salesperson who attended one of my seminars, recently ran into a situation where he had a very strong Sponsor—but the Sponsor's boss was a strong Anti-Sponsor. However, the Sponsor thought her boss was headed in the wrong direction, and therefore decided to quietly work around him. Why was she willing to take this risk? "I don't want to go down the road my boss wants to go down, because I'm going to be responsible for implementation," she said. "I don't want this project to fail." Because she had credibility with the West Coast president and knew that *he* had access to her boss's boss, she suggested that Kurt approach the West Coast president and ask for a meeting. This Sponsor has a business goal of helping her company improve efficiency, and a personal goal of wanting to advance her career, wanting to achieve a big personal win instead of an embarrassing loss.

Configurations of a Complex Buying Team

Every member of a Complex Buying Team will have a unique combination of interests and roles. Similarly, every Complex Buying Team is unique because the players can come together in many different configurations. Often one person will be representing more than one perspective—an Integrator who is also a User, for example. Sometimes more than one person will fill a particular role. Many teams will, for example, include multiple Users. Sample configurations are shown in Figure 2-6.

Notice that the diagram reflects the dual role of Power Brokers: they are almost always someone who has some other purpose for being on the team—a User, an Integrator, a Gatekeeper, or the ROI Authority. Obviously, one of your first jobs when selling to a Complex Buying Team is to figure out the members, their interests, and their relative power or influence.

A Case Study in Complex Buying Team Dynamics

At the beginning of this chapter I mentioned an instance where I ended up losing a second and larger sale even though a first sale

Figure 2-6 Sample Configurations of a Buying Team

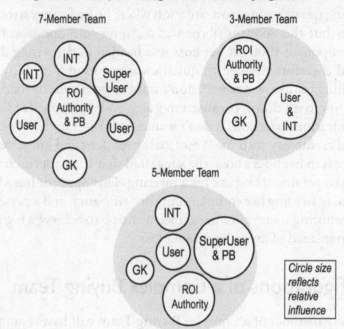

7-Member Team

INT
INT
Super User
ROI Authority & PB
User
User
GK

3-Member Team

ROI Authority & PB
GK
User & INT

5-Member Team

INT
User
SuperUser & PB
GK
ROI Authority

Circle size reflects relative influence

(and the subsequent training delivery) had gone smoothly. That experience is a perfect example of why you need to pay attention to all the players on a Complex Buying Team and especially how you deal with Sponsors and Anti-Sponsors. Here's more detail on what happened:

Acting upon a referral, I had contacted Norm, the vice president of sales for a New York City–based company that operates, installs, and designs data management systems for financial institutions. Norm said he and his regional sales managers had just concluded they needed to provide sales training for their fifty major-account sales representatives and were about to begin evaluating options. (I also learned, incidentally, that the company had an additional 150 regional sales reps.)

Perfect timing! I had located a prospect who had just arrived at Step 3, *Research*. Norm said he would be delegating the project to Patricia, his San Francisco–based regional sales manager who, he told me, would be "doing the legwork," looking for the optimal sales training solution. I met with Patricia, who was the Power Broker and Gatekeeper; I assumed Norm was the ROI Authority.

I followed my usual sales process, meeting with a representative User (one of Patricia's direct reports), then meeting again with Patricia to confirm and expand on the User needs (Sales Role 2, Doctor), while at the same time designing a solution that both met these needs and locked out my two competitors (Sales Role 3, Architect). Patricia eventually became a strong Sponsor for my cause after comparing my solution to several competitors, and she reported this to Norm. I was ultimately awarded the contract.

A few weeks before we delivered the training, Patricia called and asked me to expedite information regarding my company and our training program to Jim, her company's vice president of Marketing. This was the first time I'd heard about Jim. Patricia said Jim was upset with her because training was part of Marketing's budget (making Jim the actual ROI Authority), and he had not been consulted on the decision to hire a sales training provider. She commented that I was caught in a power struggle between Jim and Norm, marketing versus sales. Uh-oh. I quickly sent the information to Jim, and followed up with a couple of phone calls, but never got a response.

Still, the original training went through and a few weeks later, my associates and I delivered our training program to a group of fifty major-account salespeople. The program received rave reviews. Jim attended, and even joined me for lunch, during which he was very positive about what he was seeing. Naturally, I felt confident about winning the next, much larger contract.

A few weeks later, I learned that Norm had been fired. (Jim had obviously won the power struggle.) Ouch! Jim took control of the decision to train the larger group of 150 salespeople, and once again did not return my calls. He met with three training companies, none of which was mine, despite our in-depth knowledge of his company's needs acquired from our first training engagement, proven record of success, and enthusiastic support that we had from the other regional sales managers.

Patricia had lost credibility as a Sponsor and the VP of Sales was gone, so even though I had strong support from other regional managers, I had no influence with Jim. He had become an Anti-Sponsor. My "sure thing" second sale was in big trouble.

How did it all turn out? Everybody lost. I lost the sale. The sales training program that Jim selected didn't make it past the initial pilot stage. It lacked support from the field sales managers, who were upset that a sales training decision had been made without their involvement. Jim lost credibility with both the president and the field sales managers, because time and money were wasted on an ineffective pilot training program. Eventually, he lost control of all sales training decisions. The sales force lost because the training project was postponed for eighteen months, until well after a new vice president of sales was hired.

What I learned from this experience is that internal politics can scuttle "sure thing" sales, so I needed to become more sensitive to internal struggles. Second, I learned to ask a vital question of all potential clients as a way to help me identify the true ROI Authority: **Whose budget is at stake?**

How to Avoid the Biggest Mistakes

There are many ways to lose a complex sale simply due to the difficulties of juggling multiple players in different stages of the buy-learning process. So the first step in mastering the politics of selling to a Complex Buying Team is to avoid the common big mistakes.

Mistake #1. Dancing Only with the One Who Brung Ya!

I've seen it happen hundreds of times. A salesperson has a great meeting with a contact at a potential customer, comes away full of confidence, and thereafter continues to groom only that one contact. (They are assuming the sale is simple and believe their one contact can "make it happen." A natural human tendency is to want to simplify that which is complex.)

In a complex sale, your single most powerful weapon other than relationships is going to be information. Because, by definition, many people are involved in a complex sale, you won't have a full arsenal if you only contact one person. You need to get to a second decision maker—and then get to a third and fourth and fifth. When you slow down and take the time to seek out additional decision makers, you will learn more about the customer's true needs, knowledge you can use to help your customer buy faster.

Mistake #2. Assuming the Complex Buying Team Has Clearly Defined Its Needs

Your ability to win a sale will rest in large part on your ability to fully understand your customers' needs. But don't for a minute think that your customers are doing a good job of defining those needs themselves. Michael M. Lombardo and Robert W. Eichinger's leadership book *FYI: For Your Improvement, A Guide for Development and Coaching* cites research from a number of different studies. The finding: 90 percent of the problems of middle managers and above are ambiguous. It's neither clear what the real problem is, nor what the solution ought to be. And the higher up the organization someone goes the more ambiguous the issues are.[7]

This ambiguity means that **the various players on a Complex Buying Team are probably defining both the problem and the solution in different ways.** You can make this lack of clarity work to your advantage if you can gain access to multiple members of the team, and use that access to help the customer recognize that different people are seeing the problem or opportunity in different ways—and then resolve the ambiguity so they have a more vivid, complete picture of their situation and a deeper understanding of their problems or opportunities. Your inside knowledge will significantly improve your odds of winning the sale, because nine times out of ten the salesperson who wins is the one who defines the customer's true problem.

Mistake #3: Going to the C-Level with Nothing to Say

Today's sales literature is chock full of titles on how to sell to the "chief" whatever (CEO, CFO, CIO, C-anything). The unfortunate consequence is that too many salespeople are so focused on getting to a higher level that they have nothing valuable to say when they get there. They can't talk with credibility because they don't have an in-depth understanding of the customer's business problems.

Contrary to popular belief, therefore, if you have a productive meeting with the first decision maker, **the next most logical step may be to go** *down* **the organizational chart to the User level in order to define/observe the need in action.** Getting this kind of firsthand knowledge of the customer's problem at the User level is what will help you be more persuasive at the C-level. This is also a good way to identify additional needs the customer may not be aware of. (More on this in the next chapter.)

Mistake #4: Antagonizing Gatekeepers

A Gatekeeper typically will view it as his or her job to prevent you from "bothering" other members of the Complex Buying Team. If you try to ride roughshod over administrative Gatekeepers or try to work around *any* Gatekeeper, you can make things worse.

Keep in mind that Gatekeepers are playing a vital role from the customers' viewpoint. You don't want to tick them off, get them mad, or have them prevent your access to other players on the team. My best advice is to treat every Gatekeeper, no matter their rank or position, as you would a C-level executive. Don't be pushy.

If a Gatekeeper is more an obstruction than a pathway to infor-mation, you might be tempted to try to go *around* him or her, but going around a Gatekeeper backfires more often than it helps. So you have to develop strategies for working *with* Gatekeepers (not against them) in ways that preserve their role but still gives you ac-cess to the people and information you need.

There are several ways to do this. One option is to **ask the Gate-keeper questions that he or she can't answer.** For example, Jack sells package delivery services. Usually he first approaches a freight manager who ends up being a User-Gatekeeper on the buying team. Freight managers are concerned about the costs of *outgoing* goods, not *incoming* goods, and Jack's services address both types of costs. So he asks the freight manager about production and warehousing of in-bound materials. Since the freight manager can't answer those questions, Jack gets referrals to manufacturing executives. He has gotten past the Gatekeeper.

If the questions you ask are important to understanding the prospect's need, hopefully you'll get the Gatekeeper's permission to seek out the person who has the answers. The sooner in the buying process you do this, the greater the likelihood of your being referred to the C-level.

A second option is to offer to work on behalf of the Gatekeeper by **gathering information from other people and then reporting back to him or her with your findings.** You can also ask the Gatekeeper if he or she wants to accompany you on the interviews with the other members of the team.

A third option is to **sell your Gatekeeper on the benefits of involving higher-level decision makers.** Unless your Gatekeeper controls the budget or has fiscal responsibility, for example, valid questions about financial factors may get you referred to someone higher up in the food chain.

Looking Ahead

Whenever you know, or even just suspect, that more than one person is involved in a sale that you're pursuing, you want to identify as many players on the buying team as you can. That information will be critical to developing a winning strategy, as I discuss in the next chapter.

CHAPTER 3

Winning the Complex Sale

Margaret sells software that reduces by half the process time needed to develop promotional materials (emails, ads, etc.) and lets her clients more easily target many more specific customer segments. The product is used primarily by large retailers and solves ingrained communication difficulties between their marketing, advertising, and retailing/merchandising departments. To sell this product effectively, Margaret's strategy is to approach each department individually to help them recognize how *their* department will be better off by supporting Margaret's software solution.

As Margaret has learned, when dealing with a Complex Buying Team you have to keep in mind that **each individual has his or her own buying process and buying criteria,** influenced by personal self-interest and the interests of their departments. At any given moment, it's likely that different decision makers will be at a different step of the buying process.

To win a complex sale, you will need the ability to not just identify who the players are (as described in Chapter 2), but also to develop a strategy that takes into account all the players and where each is in his or her buying process. Here, "slowing down" means learning to pay attention to all members of a Complex Buying

Team, so you can develop more relationships and gain access to information that your competitors won't have.

This chapter talks about the big picture of selling to a Complex Buying Team: questions to ask, fundamental skills to master, and political skills to sharpen. It provides the broader context for applying the individual sales roles described in Part II.

The Questions You Can't Afford Not to Ask

Any time you are working with a Complex Buying Team, you need to determine what factors are working for you in the sale, what factors are working against you, and what you can do to put yourself in a better position to win. Those insights will come by asking questions such as:

1. **Who will be involved in this decision? What step are they at in their buying process?** One buying influencer could be in the *Comparison* step, convinced of the need, having already identified decision criteria, and ready to compare options. Another buying team member could be questioning whether or not the need is significant enough to justify doing anything at all.

2. **Who are the most influential decision makers? At what stages of the buying process will they be involved?** The various members of the buying team have different levels of influence on the decision, which can be asserted either throughout the buying process or only at a few steps. (As was the case with Patricia's boss in Chapter 2, the C-level is usually active at the early stage but then backs out, delegating power and influence to the Power Broker.)

3. **What does each decision maker want? What are his or her problems/needs?** You need to identify what it is that each decision maker wants. Factors you'll need to look at will include how each decision maker's job performance is measured, a good clue as to what that buying team member would

want to get out of this investment. Other factors include what specific problems each decision maker has that your product/service can solve and how your solution will do a better job of solving those problems than your competitors' solutions.

4. **What is the attitude of the most influential decision makers about your company and its solution?** How do these individuals perceive your organization, your solutions, and your people? Have they had a positive experience with you before? Or with one of your competitors? Have they had a negative experience with you? With your competitors?

You will be able to get answers to many of these questions simply by asking these exact questions to the person who becomes your main Sponsor. You'll have to pursue other answers more indirectly, ideally by getting access to as many other members of the Complex Buying Team as you can.

Fundamental Skills to Master

In a complex sale, the vast majority of the sale takes place when you're not there, when individuals on the buying team communicate with each other. Therefore, you want the people on a Complex Buying Team to be selling your solution to each other. And that requires that you learn how to identify and deal with each type of player. Key skills you should master are how to:

1. Get to multiple decision makers quickly.
2. Identify what is important to each player.
3. Know where each player is in the buying process.

Skill #1: Getting to Multiple Decision Makers Quickly

It should be obvious that you will have more insights into your prospect's decision-making process and be more persuasive overall if you connect to as many people involved in the decision as soon as possible. Having information from multiple decision makers is going to make the difference in *how* you sell.

➤ In particular, try to get to the ROI Authority at the beginning of the sale. This is important for two reasons: (1) As I'll discuss in detail later in this chapter, the ROI Authority may drop out soon after you enter the picture and you may not see him or her again until the very end, and (2) access will be harder once a Gatekeeper is put in place.

➤ Although many times the people making a major purchasing decision are *not* the Users, ultimately it will be the Users who have to implement the change. Your justifications about why your solution is the best choice will have more sway if you can demonstrate a thorough understanding of User needs (as well as those of the other decision makers).

Another reason to get to as many people as *quickly* as you can is that you won't know up front who is the ROI Authority, the Power Broker, the key Users, and so on (in fact, the team may not have even been formed yet). Making contact with many people will increase the odds that you'll get to one or more of these players early in their decision process. It will help you scope out which people are interested in what issues, and also how power is playing out on the team (which will direct you toward the Power Broker). **In a complex sale, the sooner you know what you don't know—and therefore need to learn—the better.**

Skill #2: Addressing What Is Important to Each Player

As discussed in Chapter 2, every player on a team will have different interests—and some will have multiple interests if they are playing multiple roles. The skill you have to develop is how to use that information to help them understand the WIIFM (what's in it for me) of your solution.

For example, Margaret, the software sales rep introduced at the beginning of this chapter, normally makes initial contact with the

VP of marketing. Her next stop is the merchandising department. Why? For Margaret's software to reduce the cycle time to develop new ads, the merchandising department must make a significant change in operations and actually do more work up front. The thought of having to do more work up front can turn the merchandising department into an Anti-Sponsor of her solution. To head off that resistance, she gets to the merchandising department quickly and helps them see how they will be better off: The additional upfront work will make it easier for them to produce more effective and profitable ads, and prevent many of the problems they currently experience very late in the process.

This early access by Margaret helps her manage the message. She is able to discuss the problems that merchandising has that her software solves. This communicates the value proposition before anyone on the inside can start spreading the opinion that "the company is considering software that will increase your workload." This has helped her effectively prevent many Anti-Sponsor threats.

Skill #3: Knowing Where Each Player Is in the Buying Process

As mentioned earlier, various members of the Complex Buying Team will be at different steps in the buy-learning process at any given moment in time. Figure 3-1 shows some examples.

> The ROI Authority will often back out after Step 2, *Discontent*— and stay in the background until the team is ready to make a recommendation. He or she essentially remains in the Need phase (*Change* or *Discontent* step) until brought back into the process when a decision is about to be made. **This is one**

Figure 3-1 Team Members in Different Steps of Buying

ROI Authority	Power Broker	User 1	User 2	Integrator	Gate-keeper
Discontent	Research	Comparison	Change	Research	Comparison

reason why price sensitivity emerges so late in the sale— the person whose budget is at stake has just reappeared on the stage and may just be learning about the actual cost.

➤ Users can be in many different stages. Some Users can be further along in their buying process than other decision makers, especially if they alerted the others to the need in the first place (see User 1 in Figure 3-1). Other Users may just have become aware that the problem is being addressed (see User 2 in Figure 3-1). Still other Users may be resistant to change of any kind.

➤ An Integrator doesn't typically get involved until Step 3, *Research* (after a need has been recognized), to identify technical criteria and to ensure that the options considered will mesh with the rest of the organization.

➤ A Gatekeeper often isn't appointed until sometime between Step 3, *Research*, and Step 4, *Comparison*. (Sometimes, but not always, the Gatekeeper is the User who helped identify the problem and is furthest along in the buying process, as is the case in Figure 3-1.)

➤ A Power Broker will often move more deliberately through the process, sometimes lagging behind other decision makers but usually ahead of the ROI Authority. He or she is often a consensus builder who is sounding out the opinions of others—and upon finding the goals and attitudes of others in conflict, may be more cautious.

Recognizing that different people are in different steps will help you better match your selling behavior to their buying needs. A buyer in Step 2, *Discontent*, needs help in recognizing a problem and its seriousness (the Doctor role). A buyer in Step 3, *Research*, needs help in designing a solution (the Architect role). A buyer in Step 4, *Comparison*, needs proof that you're the best choice (the Coach role). A buyer in Step 5, *Fear*, needs you to draw out some fears and help to resolve them (the Therapist role).

There's a big secret to finding out what step a decision maker is in: **Simply ask, "Where are you in your decision-making**

process?" It's unlikely they'll answer using the terminology introduced in this book ("Well, Kevin, I'm moving out of *Discontent* into the *Research* step"). But they'll use other phrases that can give you valuable clues: "We've just started the process" (*Discontent*) . . . "We've studied the problem and are now defining what we should do" (*Research*) . . . "We have to present our management with three competing proposals by next week" (deep into *Comparison*). Other indicators are covered in each of the sales roles chapters; you can also ask your Sponsor to help you make this determination.

When in the Buying Process to Reach Each Decision Maker

When dealing with Complex Buying Teams, knowing who the players are and how they interact with each other are two key factors. A third is understanding that different members of the team will be more or less active depending on what phase of the buying process they are in. For example:

> The ROI Authority for most major purchases is likely a C-level executive who will be most actively involved early in the buying process, during the Need stage, to help understand the issues and set objectives. In their book, *Selling to the C-Suite*, authors Read and Bistritz interviewed more than sixty senior executives, ranging from vice presidents to chairmen, from a variety of industries, and found that 80 percent were involved at the beginning steps of a buying process to understand the issues and set objectives. But then the C-level backs out and for the most part delegates the establishment of criteria and evaluation of options to the lower-level personnel who are closer to the situation. The authors cite an executive who said, "I get involved in the *what* and *why*, not so much the *how*."[8] **This means that if you want to sell to the C-level you need to be involved early in the buying decision,** in order to help your client better recognize their problems and define their needs.

> At least some Users, particularly those with greater levels of influence, will typically be involved throughout the buying process. The User level is often where the problems (or at least the symptoms) are first recognized by the customer.

> The Integrator, as the expert who establishes the technical buying criteria that must be met by individual suppliers, typically becomes involved after a need has been defined during the *Research* step. Then he or she evaluates the match between various suppliers and the technical criteria during the *Comparison* step.

> Usually, the Gatekeeper is not appointed until the *Comparison* step, because that's when the process could become a burden on decision makers (if multiple vendors are trying to contact them directly). That means if *you* initiated the sales opportunity, you are likely entering the buying process in the *Change* or *Discontent* step of the buying process, before the Gatekeeper appears on the scene, and will often have direct access to at least some decision makers. If you are brought in later in the buying process, you will likely have to work through a Gatekeeper.

Matching Your Selling to the Buying Team's Dynamics

Figure 3-2 summarizes the information above into a typical pattern of how decision makers come and go during the buying decision. Consider this map as a general guideline, subject to change depending on how your prospect operates. You will certainly encounter exceptions to the flow of events I depict. But this map can give you a starting point for strategizing about which decision makers you need to contact at each phase of the buy-learning process.

Here is a description of what is happening with the buying team in each step of the process shown in Figure 3-2 and what the salesperson should be doing in response:

Step 1: *Change.* Users and Super Users will likely be the first people to notice change is happening, because they struggle with the impact on their jobs every day. You need to understand the changes affect-

Figure 3-2 When Different Decision Makers Are Most Active

	1. Change	2. Discontent	3. Research	4. Comparison	5. Fear	6. Commitment	7. Expectation	8. Satisfaction
ROI Authority		X				X		X
Power Broker			X	X	X	X	X	X
Super User	X	X	X	X	X	X	X	X
User (hands on)	X	X	X				X	X
Integrator			X	X			X	
Gatekeeper				X	X			

ing your prospect company and how those changes will, over time, intensify the seriousness of the customer's discontent.

Step 2: *Discontent*. Talk with a User (or preferably Super User, an upper-level manager in a department) to uncover their problems and issues, so you can diagnose their needs. Then persuade that User to schedule a meeting between them, you, and the ROI Authority so you can share your diagnosis. If you can't get in to see the ROI Authority, then ask who he or she delegates to. Who is the ROI Authority's "trusted lieutenant"? Try to meet with that person (likely to become the Power Broker).

Step 3: *Research*. As noted above, the ROI Authority typically moves to the background at or before this step, delegating the responsibility for learning and evaluation of options to someone who is mostly likely the Power Broker. The Power Broker, in turn, seeks out the Integrator (the technical expert), who then becomes involved in formulating technical requirements and ensuring that seamless compatibility will be achieved. Users offer suggestions on criteria that should be considered. (Hands-on Users will usually back out after that; Super Users will stay involved.) Your goal is to try to see both the Integrator and the Power Broker (not necessarily in the same meeting). **If you can't get in to see the Power Broker, go see the Integrator. Don't just "hang out" with the User!**

Step 4: *Comparison.* At this point, the Gatekeeper will usually seek you out and say, "From here on out, go through me." If this person is an influential decision maker, not just someone who is screening calls, he or she will likely be meeting with your competitors during this step. At the sales presentation/proposal meeting the Power Broker runs the show. The Integrator and Gatekeeper are almost always in attendance. Hands-on Users are often not involved because the company wants them at their desks being productive, and may not want them to know the details of the investment being considered. Consider yourself lucky if the ROI Authority shows up at your sales presentation.

Anti-Sponsors often become visible at your presentation as they pepper you with questions. You have two choices. If their bias is personal/subjective, try and draw them into an objective discussion of their needs in front of the group. (There's an example of this strategy in the next section.) Another alternative is to ask, "Would you mind staying after this meeting is over so you and I can discuss this?" This prevents the Anti-Sponsor from derailing your sales presentation.

Step 5: *Fear.* As doubts and fears creep in, this is a crucial time to maintain communication with your Sponsor to probe what's going on behind closed doors. Ideally, you will follow the advice given later in this book about finding a reason to meet with decision makers following the presentation (see Chapter 8).

Step 6: *Commitment.* The Power Broker or the purchasing manager spearheads the negotiation. You must be prepared with your most convincing justifications to persuade the customer that you are their best choice.

Step 7: *Expectations*. This is the implementation phase, where the Integrator reigns supreme. Technical compatibility must be achieved. Users reenter because they're the ones who must learn to operate your solution, and in so doing, change the way they do things. Make sure you have their support, because if you don't they can sabotage the implementation. The Power Broker stays involved because this is the first feedback on the success of his or her leadership efforts. Failure here can be very embarrassing for the Power Broker.

Step 8: *Satisfaction*. The ROI Authority is curious about the ROI. What results were achieved with this investment? Now is your opportunity to gain access to this person, and build a relationship that you can "farm" for months and years to come.

Sharpening Your Political Skills

To win a complex sale, you must be a savvy strategist. Two of the most important strategies to master are how to defuse a threat from an Anti-Sponsor and how to create credibility at the C-level.

Neutralizing a Threat from an Anti-Sponsor

There is a human tendency to avoid confrontation. But the greatest threat to winning a complex sale is the person who doesn't want to buy from you, the Anti-Sponsor. The most successful strategy for neutralizing an Anti-Sponsor is being proactive. Identify who is against you, assess that person's power and influence on the decision, and take action to defuse the threat.

Here's an example of how that works: Juanita sells wireless devices that help companies track the productivity of their field personnel. Juanita was on a phone call with the VP of manufacturing (a strong Sponsor) a few days prior to a sales presentation, and asked if there was anyone scheduled to be in the meeting who might be opposed to her company's solution. (It's a question you should ask of your Sponsor before every sales presentation. Opinions are changeable during the course of a complex buying decision, often due to your competitors' sales efforts.) There was a moment of silence, then the VP said, "Well, our director of IT has endorsed one of your competitors."

Because she learned about this potential threat ahead of time, Juanita was prepared. Early in her presentation, she turned to the IT director and asked him directly, "What are your criteria for making this decision?" The IT guy named a handful of criteria, which Juanita captured on a flipchart for all to see. Juanita then walked through each one of those criteria and showed how her company's solution met or exceeded each one. By bringing the Anti-Sponsor's criteria out in a group setting, Juanita was able to show that she could effectively meet those needs. The Anti-Sponsor's personal bias against Juanita's solution was greatly diminished, at least in the eyes of the other decision makers, and she won the sale.

Going Down the Corporate Ladder Before Going Up

In *Selling to the C-Suite*, Nicholas Read and Stephen Bistritz say that the most effective way to gain access to the executive level is through an internal referral: 84 percent of executives said they would "usually or always" grant a meeting with a salesperson who was referred internally. Cold calling ranked lowest; only 20 percent of executives say they would grant a meeting.[9]

That finding represents a dilemma for those of you who have been reading book after book that tells you to get to the C-level as quickly as possible. Here is another case where you run into the paradox of modern selling described in Chapter 2: **The best way to get to the C-level may be to go down the corporate ladder before you go up it.** Why? Because going down gives you a better understanding of the company's needs and challenges, and provides you with more ammunition to use when you talk to an executive.

Let's say, for example, that you were successful in scheduling an initial meeting with a Super User, the head of a department. Your meeting is going well, and the prospect shows some real interest. So you ask, "Who else would you need to talk to about this?" The Super User tells you that the COO's support is critical because she controls the budget at stake.

Rather than immediately request a meeting with the COO, you make a two-part request of the Super User: first, that you be allowed to go *down* to a lower level to observe and further diagnose the need, and second, that you then be scheduled to report back with your findings in a meeting with both the Super User and COO.

The Super User will likely agree with this proposal if you've met two criteria: First, you have helped the Super User realize the value of addressing the issue now. Second, the Super User is confident that your focus in the meeting with the COO will be on problem diagnosis and *not* pitching your product. Under those conditions, it is in the Super User's self-interest to have you meet with the COO as an outside expert (who has experience with similar issues in other companies), and have you share your firsthand observations about their company.

Winning Over a Complex Buying Team Takes Skill

Winning a complex sale is difficult. Complex sales are bigger-ticket sales, and because your competition wants them as much as you do, success takes more than simple desire and a strong will. Winning also takes sales strategies and tactics that are more effective than those of your competitors. And, in the end, the positive impact your solution achieves for the customer is your most important differentiator.

Complex sales are also difficult because each decision maker has his or her own buy-learning process. What you need to learn is how to help each person complete each step of the process better and faster. The sales consulting roles described in the following chapters provide a game plan for persuading each decision maker to give you and your solution a thumbs-up.

PART II

The Eight Roles of
Buying-Focused Selling

How to Get Started with the Eight Sales Roles

While it's important to understand why and how people buy, that's not enough to automatically help you win more sales. You also need to have a plan that addresses what's most important to each decision maker at each step of their buying process.

The structure of Part II is patterned after the buy-learning process introduced in Chapter 1, and reproduced in the figure on the next page. There are eight chapters in this section of the book, one for each step of the buy-learning process. The first portion of each chapter describes one step of the customer's buying process. The second portion describes the **matching sales role**.

As I described in Chapter 1, the sales roles—student, doctor, architect, coach, therapist, negotiator, teacher, farmer—capture what you can do as a salesperson to help the customer through each buying step. Understanding this match is what will help you deliver a winning plan.

These chapters serve the purpose of helping you answer three questions:

The Sales Wheel

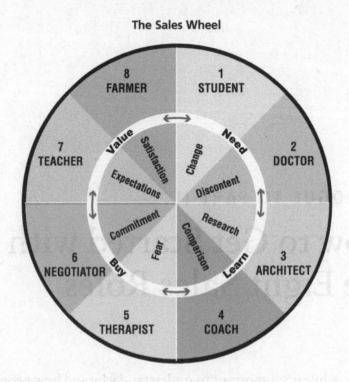

1. Where is each decision maker in the buying process?
2. What role should I adopt in order to move an individual to the next step?
3. What specific action do I want my prospect to take at the end of the next meeting, and by when?

In short, I want to help you get better at spotting the step of buying your customer is in, and pick out actions you can take to help them make it to the *next* step most efficiently and effectively.

While having to learn eight separate steps of buying and eight roles that match those steps may sound daunting at first, here is a tip that has helped others: When viewed holistically, the entire buy-learning wheel is a **model for questioning**. The role names are meant to help you remember what types of questions you should be asking of yourself and of your prospect.

Adopting these roles is likely to feel awkward at first because you've probably been trained to jump into your pitch quite soon after contacting a customer. Learning to slow down and probe for the customer's needs takes time. You'll typically feel the first pangs of discomfort when you start asking second- and third-level questions. Think of the sense of awkwardness as growing pains that are going to take you to a higher skill level.

Focus on Obtaining Go-Forward Commitments

Interspersed with the eight sales roles you'll find four "milestones," checkpoints in your sales process. The milestones cover everything from getting a first appointment to delivering a presentation and transitioning to implementation. At each milestone—and, in fact, any time you have contact with a customer—I want you to think about not only what you want as an outcome, but what you want to ask your customer to do so that they will continue to move through their buying process.

Sound easy? Not so fast. In my seminars we have an exercise that asks salespeople to consider the next three appointments they have set, and then to answer the question, "What is your objective for that sales call?" The answers I received at a recent seminar fell into the following categories:

- Create a need.
- Discuss the client's marketing objectives.
- Provide an overview of our capabilities.
- Build trust with a new contact.
- Identify decision makers.
- Get a commitment to buy.

Look closely at those "objectives." How is "get a commitment to buy" different from all the others? The answer: it's the only one that requires the *customer* to take action. All the others are activities for the salesperson. To me, this is another example of how many salespeople think too much about what they're trying to do and not enough about what the customer needs to do to move forward in their buying process.

The key question to ask yourself before each sales call or meeting is, **what specific action do I want my prospect to agree to take at the end of this meeting?** To make this more real to you, think about the kinds of actions your customers take as they move through a buying process and end up purchasing and installing your product or service. Now think about where one of your current prospects is in that process and ask them for an action that will take them further along in that step or even to the next step. This is what I call a **customer go-forward commitment.**

For example, a sales team for a client who sells process control valves listed the following actions taken by their customers during a typical buying process:

> - Refers us to a second decision maker.
> - Allows us access to their company's manufacturing area to perform on-site needs analysis/measurement.
> - Invites our salesperson to meet with two other decision influencers to share findings from our needs analysis of their company.
> - Agrees to a tour of either our facilities or those of a customer who is using our control valves.
> - Agrees to call our references.
> - Attends a sales presentation.
> - Agrees to a forty-five-minute meeting with our salesperson to review the sales proposal.

The first bullet—"refers you to a second decision maker"—is the kind of action you would like a customer in Step 2, *Discontent*, to take in order to move them closer to Step 3, *Research*. The last bullet—"reviews the sales proposal"—is an action that a customer in Step 4, *Comparison*, would need to take before moving to Step 5, *Fear*, and ultimately Step 6, *Commitment*.

Also notice that each action is something the customer does.

The last bullet, for example, is not that *the salesperson* prepares a proposal. It's that *the customer* commits to a forty-five-minute meeting to review that proposal.

I'll discuss more about how to weave these objectives into your customer contact in the following chapters. In the meantime, you can start to apply this notion by thinking about your the next sales call. What is your objective for that call? Is it something *you* are going to do during the call, or something *your customer* is going to do after the call?

Once you've attained a commitment, you know your customer is taking action. They're becoming more in-

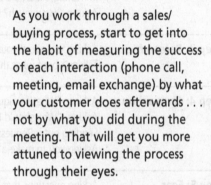

Tip: Measure Success by Your Customer's Actions

As you work through a sales/buying process, start to get into the habit of measuring the success of each interaction (phone call, meeting, email exchange) by what your customer does afterwards . . . not by what you did during the meeting. That will get you more attuned to viewing the process through their eyes.

volved. They're investing their time, energy, and brainpower into this buying decision and are showing you interest. If you are eventually going to ask the customer for a major commitment to buy, it makes sense to obtain some minor customer commitments along the way.

Getting Started

To get started applying this buying-focused sales process, do the following preparation before your next calls or appointments:

- Identify where the customer or prospect is in their buying process. The table entitled "Buying Step Indicators" on the next page summarizes some typical indicators to help you get started.

- Based on where you think the customer is, use the information in the appropriate chapter to help you make a list of *at least five questions* you want to ask that prospect, questions you would not have asked before you read this book.

Table A

BUY-LEARNING STEP	TYPICAL INDICATORS
Step 1: *Change*	Changes in the customer's industry or marketplace Changes within the customer's organization
Step 2: *Discontent*	Saying, "I wish we could . . ." Saying, "We can't . . ." Indicating, "It would be nice if . . ." Asking, "How much? What's the ballpark cost?"
Step 3: *Research*	Asking you about your solution's capabilities Talking about what their solution must or should do
Step 4: *Comparison*	Asking, "What's unique about your product or service?" Asking, "Why should I choose you?" Sending out a Request for Proposal (an RFP) Asking you to make a formal presentation
Step 5: *Fear*	Asking questions that may indicate second thoughts about purchasing Raising old concerns that had been previously resolved Sending nonverbal signals that all is not right Becoming uncommunicative Making unrealistic or inappropriate demands Postponing agreed-upon go-forward commitments
Step 6: *Commitment*	Reviewing the specifics of your contract offering Complaining that your price is too high
Step 7: *Expectation of Value*	Asking you for assistance with implementation Telling you the solution doesn't seem to work—or at least they can't make it work
Step 8: *Satisfaction*	Telling you they're satisfied and are achieving the desired results Showing proficiency with using what they've bought

> Think about what you could do during the call or meeting to move the customer to the next buying step, presuming your analysis is correct. Also, have a backup plan in case they are in a different buying step than you thought.

That's your starting point. Keep track of the new "five questions" you develop for each step of the buying process, and use them on your next customer, and the next one after that. As you become comfortable with each set, continue this procedure, gradually adding more and more questions to each role. This is what I mean by "slow down" (so you can ask more questions), and "sell faster" (because you'll do a better job of diagnosing customer needs and therefore structuring a solution that's a better fit). Developing the habit of doing this kind of preparation before each contact with a customer will greatly increase your sales effectiveness because you'll come into each call better prepared and more persuasive.

CHAPTER 4

The Student

Use Knowledge to Gain an Edge

Today, your ability to add value by serving in a consultative role is key to your sales success. To do this you must understand your customers and their environment, and how your product and services can fit into that context. Here is a story that demon-strates how the knowledge you gain from studying your customers can serve as the basis for identifying customer needs that you are uniquely qualified to address.

Lou is a salesperson for a supply chain management company that maintains more than 28 million square feet of dry and tem-perature-controlled warehouse space throughout a network of about 120 distribution hubs worldwide. Lou contacts companies in the consumer products, electronics, food and beverage, manu-facturing, and pharmaceutical industries with the goal of convinc-ing prospects that outsourcing their supply chain needs (or a portion of their supply chain) will allow them to focus more on their core business. He has to call on the equivalent of a vice pres-ident of logistics—not someone below that level (such as the warehouse manager), because his solution might eliminate that lower-level job.

Lou was interested in approaching a major beverage business headquartered in his territory. He went to the "Investor Services" section of the prospect's website, pulled up its most recent 10-K (the annual report required by the Securities and Exchange Commission that includes information such as company history, organizational structure, executive compensation, equity, subsidiaries, and audited financial statements). He went right to the section labeled "Management's Discussion of Results of Operations." First, he read that this company considered its competitive advantage to be its "integrated brand ownership, bottling, and distribution" system, which helped them be more flexible and responsive to the changing needs of large retail customers. More specifically, this business model enabled the beverage company to "coordinate sales, service, distribution, promotions, and product launches" more effectively than their competition.

Scanning further, Lou read that operating costs for the previous year took a $57-million one-time charge due to "reduction of employees in corporate, sales, and the supply chain." They had closed one of their distribution centers in the Southwest. Lou's company had significant warehouse space in the Southwest, so perhaps this was a good fit. Lou spent, in total, about twenty minutes studying the 10-K. At the end of that time, he knew that when he called the SVP, he could comment on a "pain point" or two that could have been created by last year's changes.

Lou was successful at scheduling an appointment with his prospect's SVP, and eventually made his largest sale for that quarter. The customer later told him that at the time Lou called, the customer was struggling with distribution problems in the Southwest. Sales had increased after the closure of his distribution center, which placed more pressure on his other warehouses and transportation providers. Lou was able to connect with the prospect's pain. Lou's comment that "we have a number of distribution centers in the Southwest" triggered curiosity as to where those centers were located. If Lou hadn't known about the closure of the prospect's Southwest distribution center, there's a good chance he would never have gotten the first appointment, let alone made the sale.

Study Your Customer

Change is the only constant in your customers' lives. But within change lies the opportunity to help your customer grow. To identify those opportunities, you must become a **Student** of your prospective customers.

When you were a student in school, you studied because academic achievement depended on how much you learned. In the same way, as a sales professional, your success depends on how well you do your homework. When your customers are in the *Change* step, you want to study how the changes are affecting them and look for opportunities where you can add value.

Your goal as a Student is to get the potential customer to schedule a twenty-minute appointment. That is what you're selling. Not your product or service (at least not yet—remember the lesson from Chapter 1 about "selling too fast"). You have to know enough about the change a potential customer is experiencing and the problem they could solve with your product or service to arouse their curiosity and get them to agree to talk with you further. The amount of studying it will take to do that will vary by situation, based on factors like how senior your potential contact is, the nature of the benefit you can offer, the size of the investment you'll be asking them to make, and so on. For the purposes of this chapter, we'll assume that you will be doing a fair amount of research before you even make the first prospecting call, but it may be that, for practical purposes, you do some minimal research up front and the rest after you have confirmed an appointment.

The first part of this chapter discusses the first step of your customer's buy-learning process; the second part discusses how you can find out what kinds of changes the prospect is experiencing that would create a need for your product or service.

Customer Step 1: *Change*

In the *Change* step, your prospects find that their business or personal lives are being altered by either external or internal forces. These changes create the need for new or different products and services. Indicators of the types of forces that might be driving potential customers to consider changes are shown in Figure 4-1.

Customers in the *Change* step are experiencing discomfort with their current situation. They have a vague notion that something isn't right (and may not even be labeling it as a "problem" yet) or they may think they see an opportunity that is about to pass them by. What they may not know is that there is a solution to that problem, or a way to take advantage of an opportunity. And that's where you come in.

Figure 4-1 Indicators of Companies in the *Change* Step

External Forces	Internal Forces
Changes in customer base	Strategic planning/goal setting
Government regulations	Quality initiatives
Competitors	Cost cutting
Technology	Reorganization
The economy	

How a Student Gains a Deeper Understanding of Your Customer's Business

As a Student, it is your role to:

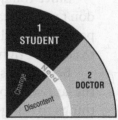

➢ **Understand the changes and pressures your prospect and their businesses are facing.** Identify changes in the company and its markets, and study how those changes are affecting your prospect to find opportunities where you can add value.

➤ **Understand the customer's decision-making hierarchy.** Determine what level of the company you normally enter, and try to move up a level or two.

The amount of time you devote to this research depends on the prospect's potential value to you. For accounts with limited potential value, your "homework" may be as simple as reviewing their website. For accounts with significant potential, your studying may involve days of analysis.

Know Three Things About Each Customer That Other Salespeople Won't Know

Before you meet with your prospect, you want to know at least three things about that person and/or their business that most salespeople wouldn't know. When you have knowledge about what your prospects do, you build instant credibility. It says, loud and clear, "I care about your business." Today's customers want to feel important, so they'd rather deal with one salesperson who understands their business than with ten salespeople who hit-and-run down the street to the next customer. Lou's research described at the beginning of this chapter, for example, let him know about specific changes his target company had recently undergone. It's what got him in the door.

Since today's buyers are busier and under more pressure, they don't want to take the time to educate salespeople about their company. They will expect salespeople to do a lot more homework just to earn the right to talk to them.

Below are some questions for focusing your research. Getting the answers to these questions can help you uncover the three things to bring out in your first meeting with the prospect:

Know about the business:

- What future changes will affect their business?
- What are the company's current goals? Strategic priorities?
- What major changes has the company recently experienced or is currently going through?
- What recent successes or failures have they seen?
- Who are the company's competitors and what are the differences between them?
- How does work flow in this business? What are the Core functions and how are they linked?
- Would you buy from this company? Why or why not?
- How can you and your company's products/services help the target business achieve its goals?

Know about the person (*some of this may not be attainable until you make contact with the company, but some of it will, especially if you're connecting with a C-level person*):

- How is this decision maker's job performance measured? The answer will reveal the prospect's personal motivations. For example, a vice president of sales wants to increase sales and gross profits; a VP of manufacturing wants to solve product quality problems and increase production levels.
- What are highlights from the person's career: jobs held in the past, education, professional affiliations, awards?
- What is this individual personally trying to accomplish?
- What changes are affecting this prospect?
- What problems does this prospect solve for his or her internal customers? External customers?
- What problems can you solve for this prospect?
- What opportunities for improvement does this prospect have that you can use to help them make a profit?

As a rule of thumb, I always recommend looking at the target company's 10-Ks (annual reports used in the United States) or Investor Reports (the label given in Canada) to read about its continuing operations (10-Qs or quarterly reports could be used as well). Plus, I research the person I'm going to be talking to: checking out their profile on LinkedIn and doing a Google search. Researching the person may uncover personal details you can use to make an associa-

> **Tip: No Time to Study?**
>
> To keep up on trends and issues in the industries you serve, read the "Letter from the Editor" in the relevant industry trade magazines. Those letters usually highlight the hot topics and emerging trends.

tion—having gone to the same college, worked for the same company, know some of the same people, and so on.

The purpose of answering these questions is so that you can talk about the concerns that keep the person you're calling awake at night or about problems that continually distract them from what they consider more valuable work. Do you know what keeps a manufacturing director up at night? Do you know what keeps a vice president of finance up at night? Knowing whatever it is that causes their insomnia will make you more effective in your approach. Here's a quick example: People selling transportation, forklifts, conveyor belts, or raw materials may be tempted to start a sales call to a manufacturing director with a generic "I can help you improve your production." But their messages will be much more powerful and effective if they can tie their product or service into specific issues concerning that person: "I see that your company experienced a significant increase in transportation costs last year...."

Sources of Information

Knowing the questions to ask is a good first step. Knowing where to find the answers is the next. **If you want to know three things about your customers that your competition doesn't know, you've got to be willing to do things that your competition won't do.**

The main source of information these days is through the Internet. Going to a company's website is an obvious step, but don't stop there. Many sites have company information and others allow you to subscribe to particular kinds of information or information about a particular sector or company. Here are just a few sources to get you started:

> LinkedIn, with its growing number of subscribers, has become a tool you can use to research both individuals you may be contacting and specific companies. For example, I recently searched for a company I was going to contact and found that someone I was connected to on LinkedIn had six connections within that target company. Working through such connections is a good way to get a personal referral that will get you past voice mail limbo.

> InsideView.com offers an online tool that monitors social networks (LinkedIn, Twitter, etc.) plus over 20,000 online news sources, then alerts you via email when an important event occurs at one of your accounts. You set the specific "trigger" events that cause you to be notified, such as the appointment of a new executive, quarterly performance report, new offerings, etc. You then have a reason for calling the prospect, which differentiates your approach from your competitors.

> Google.com/finance is a great place to start a search. Enter a company name and you'll get links to company press releases, executives, corporate history/profile, products/services, financial reports, analyst reports, etc.

> Google Alerts lets you sign up to get email notices about articles that mention companies or topics you want to track.

> Hoovers (www.hoovers.com) is a Dun & Bradstreet company that collects information about businesses, both public and private. Getting information about private companies is difficult, so Hoovers may have information you can't get elsewhere, such as a list of potential competitors. Their site profiles over 40 million companies and lists 48 million executive contacts and 8 million email addresses.

Those of you dealing with publicly traded companies can also use the Securities and Exchange Commission's "Edgar" service. To find out how to get free Edgar information, check out the tutorial at www.sec.gov/investor/pubs/edgarguide.htm (there are some companies that sell this access, but this link will show you how to get the information for free). At this site, you can read/retrieve corporate 10-K reports for all public corporations. Another source for 10-Ks and 10-Qs is the investor section on a company's website.

Corporate 10-Ks are much better than annual reports because they provide more factual information. They're written for federal regulators instead of individual investors, so the data hasn't been corrupted by spin doctors. They give a clear, concise description of what's going right—and what's going wrong—in the business, along with the company's plans for improving performance. It's exactly the information you need to get smart about your customer.

Download 10-Ks for each of your top three prospects and you'll see what I'm referring to. Remember, if you want to know three things about your customers that your competition doesn't know, you've got to be willing to do things that your competitors won't do.

Understanding the Company's Decision-Making Hierarchy

Another useful piece of information is knowing the decision-making hierarchy in a prospective business. In general, each company will have three levels of management, each caring about different types of issues (Figure 4-2):

1. At the **C-level** are senior executives whose primary focus is to look into the business's future. They're very focused on what's going to be happening one, two, or three years from now. Because their performance is measured on quarterly profitability, they listen carefully to managers of the Core functions describing the problems in their area of responsibility.

Figure 4-2 Different Concerns of Corporate Levels

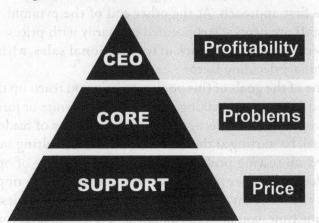

2. The middle level encompasses the **Core** business processes—
   such as manufacturing, sales, marketing, operations, and
   customer service. For your customer to gain competitive
   advantage over their rivals they must perform these Core
   functions more efficiently (at a lower cost) or more effectively
   (better) than their competition. That means solving operational
   problems. If, as the result of your sales effectiveness, you can
   help your Core-level customer to envision your solution as
   improving their company's competitiveness, the price of your
   product or service will diminish as a concern.

3. The bottom level provides **Support** for the needs of the Core
   and the C-levels and provides assistance as needed. The
   Support level includes purchasing, accounting, training, and
   the legal department. Often, the kinds of products or services
   sold at this level will be perceived as commodities, in which
   case prices will always be the overriding concern.

   Odds are that most of you reading this book will be trying to engage a prospective client, at least initially, at the Core level. While
sales at the highest levels of an organization generally represent the
largest opportunities, very few salespeople deal with the kinds of

products or service that would get them *direct* access to the C-suite on the first approach. At the other end of the pyramid, Support-level staff are generally concerned primarily with prices—meaning salespeople quickly get stuck in **transactional sales,** where price is the primary deciding factor.

One of the goals of this book is to help you reach up the corporate ladder—to start making contact at the C-suite or just below it more regularly. But I recognize that the majority of readers of this book will be starting at the Core level, where **consulting sales**—sales focused on solving problems and taking advantage of opportunities—dominate. Core problems are the kinds that have ripple effects across the company, so the pain is both acute and widespread. At the same time, you need to realize that even Core-level contacts often have to get approval for their purchases from the C-suite, so even if you're starting at the Core level you still need to frame your value propositions in ways that allow your immediate client to sell it to higher-level executives.

Aim Higher Than You Normally Would!

Since you will have greater potential the higher you go in the management levels, one key to selling faster is to target senior decision makers. As we learned in Chapter 3, internal referrals are a much more effective way (84 percent) than cold calling (20 percent) to "score" a meeting with a corporate executive.

I am all in favor of attempting to set appointments with C-suite executives, but salespeople better have something insightful to say about the organization's business problems when they show up. As mentioned in Chapter 3, you often get those insights by "studying the need in action," which is likely at the Core or Support level. Identifying those specific issues and then approaching the C-suite increases the odds of getting access through a referral and making a good impression once you get there.

Even if you can't talk to the C-suite person directly, you can sometimes leverage contact at that level to get access to lower-level people. Call the assistant of the C-level executive you've identified as responsible for the area that your product or service can help. Briefly describe the problems or challenges your product or service can help solve, and ask to whom you should speak. The goal is to have the president's or CEO's or COO's office refer you down to an appropriate senior vice president.

Put Your Knowledge to Work

Just in case you're tempted to get lazy and skip the Student work, here's a brief cautionary tale:

A salesperson I know recently emailed a regional manager he had worked with previously who had just moved to another large company. The email congratulated the regional manager on his new job, reminded him of their prior (and successful) dealings, and then asked if there was someone else in the manager's new company that the salesperson could talk to. The manager sent back a short note with a name and phone number, saying "you should talk to this guy." The salesperson immediately called the number and left a voice mail with a generic benefit statement. Only afterwards did he discover that the person he called was the COO of the company. He never got a response.

The lesson this salesperson learned was that minimally he should have asked his original contact for ten minutes to discuss any problems or issues the company was having. He also should have done research on the name he was provided before leaving an ineffective phone message and losing out on the opportunity to make a good first impression.

You can gauge the effectiveness of your work as a Student by how successful you are at grabbing a prospect's attention as you reach the first sales milestone—getting that first appointment. And that's what I'll talk about next.

MILESTONE #1

Getting More
First Appointments

D uring the final stages of finishing this book, I was supposed to
call my editor, but was running ten minutes late for our appointment. When the phone rang, I thought it was she, so I
answered the phone. A young lady said her name then immediately launched into a sales pitch. I think she was selling some sort
of "learning system"—whatever that meant. I didn't quite catch
what she was saying because my mind was still on the task I was
trying to finish up so I could begin the other call I was supposed
to be making.

She mentioned a few benefits, then began rattling off names of
well-known companies who were clients of her company. That's
when I interrupted. "Wait. Stop," I said. "This is not a good time for
me. I have another conference call."

"Then why did you pick up the phone?" she asked.

"Excuse me?" I said, astonished.

"If you had a conference call scheduled, why did you pick up the
phone just now?"

"Young lady, you need to go back into training," I said politely, then hung up the phone.

I'm going to assume that you can pick out the biggest flaw this saleswoman made: rudeness is never a good way to win a client. I hope that you will have good manners when you call prospects.

But here's a harder challenge: did you notice her other mistakes? I'm not going to tell you just yet what they are. I'd like you to read through the rest of this milestone chapter then come back and look again at what she said and did and think of *at least* two other things she should have done differently besides being polite.

There's an old saying you probably know: "You don't get a second chance to make a good first impression." What I want to do here is provide some pointers on how you can make a better first impression than you do today, and convert that goodwill into more first appointments.

The Goal: A Twenty-Minute Appointment

The Student's goal is to get a twenty-minute appointment with a potential customer. (If your meeting goes well, ideally it will last longer than twenty minutes, but that's all to ask for.) The more senior the executive you're approaching, the more difficult it's going to be to get that appointment. The place to start? Ask yourself: "Which decision maker is most negatively affected by not having already implemented my solution?"

In your initial approach to prospects, you need to create enough interest that they will be willing to talk to you for at least a minute to two, time you can use to win their agreement to a twenty-minute meeting. You can make prospects curious about what you have to say by communicating your knowledge (gained as a Student) about their specific concerns and issues.

Today, the most common method of approaching prospects is via telephone, and making effective sales calls will be the main focus on this milestone. However, look for a tip later on about how to use appointment letters.

Tip: What About In-Person Cold Calls?

For years, I recommended doing in-person cold calls because I personally found them very effective. But times have changed and in-person cold calls absolutely do not work in many settings because of security measures. Often you will simply not be able to get in the door.

However, if your "beat" includes offices where you can get in the door and speak directly with a receptionist, I urge you to give them a try. My favorite approach was always to do cold calls on a rainy day or Friday afternoons. Rainy days because it gets you sympathy. Friday because the receptionists are more likely to be in a good mood.

A Telephone Approach That Gets Results

One of our clients is a leader in reprographics, offering a comprehensive array of digital printing, computer-aided design, and reprographic solutions. To generate new business opportunities, members of their sales staff naturally sell the newest solution in the company's product line. At this moment, their "new idea" product can take project management documents, drawings, and images, replicate them electronically, and allow real-time collaboration by users anywhere in the world.

When I arrived on the scene, here is the script that they were using to call prospective clients in the commercial construction industry. My analysis is interleaved with their script:

Good afternoon, Mr. Prospect. Jeannette Jones with ABC Digital. Do you have a few minutes? *("Few minutes" is nonspecific and will likely alarm a busy prospect. Are you asking for three minutes or thirty minutes?)*

We have been helping leading project owners, managers, and key stakeholders *(Better to use the title of the person you are calling; "stakeholder" sounds like dinner)* communicate with each other by offering a web-enabled collaboration tool that allows them to share information regardless of location or time. *(You risk losing the prospect's attention right here by leading with a feature, which is not a customer problem.)*

This has helped them avoid costly mistakes, downtime, and legal troubles, and helped them by streamlining their process. *(Pretty good start, but every issue here—costly mistakes, downtime, and legal troubles—is nebulous, as is "streamlining their process." Why not replace them with construction industry jargon?)*

Can we meet for twenty minutes to introduce you to our unique offering that many organizations in your industry are implementing or researching right now? *("Can we?" suggests a lack of confidence, pleading for a meeting. It's good that Jeannette specified just twenty minutes, but it begs the question "organizations like who?" are implementing this? Drop a few names to create a "bandwagon" effect.)*

There is another problem with this script. When you talk about benefits, you connect with a small portion of your prospect "pool"— at best, about 2 percent—who are actively seeking the benefits you offer at the time that you call. The other 98 percent are living with one or more of the problem(s) and haven't yet recognized the need to find a solution, perhaps feeling a vague discontent. When you're first making contact with a customer, therefore, you can't assume they are looking for the kind of solutions you offer (and therefore would be interested in benefits).

However, if you've done your homework, you *will* know the kinds of problems they may be facing. So you'll do a better job of creating curiosity in prospects if you follow what I call the **shotgun problem statement** format: mentioning two or three problems you think they will have. That will help increase the chances of connecting with the largest portion of prospects you call on. (I like to name three problems in a shotgun statement when possible, but on a phone call you may have time to mention only two.)

The CPAs of an Effective Call

I'll get to my recommended rewrite of the above calling script in just a bit. First I want to explain the principle behind what I did. The

Tip: Using the "Shotgun" Approach Wisely

When *you* call a prospect who is not expecting your call, the odds are that he or she is in the earliest steps of the buying process—*Change* or *Discontent*. The shotgun problem statement you offer is intended to connect to problems the prospect is currently living with daily on the job.

But when a prospect seeks out information about you—perhaps by entering a search term in a search engine or calling you—they have passed the *Need* phase of the buying process. They already know, or think they know, what their problems are, and are actively looking for a solution. They are, by definition, at least in the *Research* or perhaps the *Comparison* step of the Learn phase.

However, you might be able to put a shotgun problem statement to good use. Here's an example. When visitors come to my company's website, it's likely they already think they need sales training or sales management training. But once on our site, they are offered a free report called "The 10 Biggest Mistakes Sales Managers Make." This report is a "shotgun" marketing piece that names a lot of challenges sales managers deal with and the *causes* of those symptoms. It's our way of moving a customer who is in the *Learn* phase back into the *Need* phase so we can help them define their discontent in more specific terms.

structure of my reworked version follows what I call the CPAs of an effective telephone approach:

1. **C**ourtesy
2. **P**roblem
3. **A**ction

Courtesy. Prospects are busy people. When you first call them, they are preoccupied and are not expecting your call. Therefore, your acknowledgment/greeting should be focused on a question that grabs attention. When your prospects answer the phone, *greet them by name and acknowledge that you're aware he or she is a busy person.* This will break their preoccupation with whatever they were doing when you called them. (If you don't refocus their attention, the problem statement that follows will likely fall on deaf ears.)

For me, the most effective acknowledgment statement is, "Hello, Mr. Jones, this is Kevin Davis with TopLine Leadership. Are you in a meeting or do you have just sixty seconds for me?" If the prospect is in a meeting I'll ask for a convenient time to call back.

Frequently they'll say, "Well, what have you got?" or "I've only got one minute." Either one of these responses opens the door for me to continue.

Problem. Once you have the prospect's attention, make a clear, concise statement of the problems that you solve for customers. Think about **what problems you can help the prospect solve.**

> You need to customize it not only to your prospect's industry, but also to that person's self-interest.

> Make your problem statement specific; specificity builds interest. Use the knowledge you gained in your research and use jargon or language that will resonate with the prospect (see my rewrite of Jeannette's script, next page, for an example).

Action. You must be clear and specific about the action you are asking for. What do you want your prospect to do? In this case, you want the potential customer to agree to a twenty-minute appointment.

If it's an executive and you want the prospect to agree to a specific time for an appointment, you might say: "May I see you next Tuesday at 1:45?" Once you've obtained a commitment, stop talk-

---

Tip: Put Yourself in Your Customer's Shoes

When was the last time you bought something over the phone from someone who called you out of the blue? Keep that in mind when you call your prospects. Be very clear that the only decision required is to agree to a twenty-minute meeting. Assure your prospect you'll "be brief, be interesting, and be gone."

ing: Get the appointment, say "thank you," and hang up. Don't talk past the sale.

A Revised Telephone Script

Here's how I rewrote Jeannette's phone call text based on the CPA approach, including my commentary:

Good afternoon, Mr. Prospect. This is Jeannette Jones with ABC Digital. Are you in a meeting, or do you have just sixty seconds for me? *(This breaks the prospect's concentration. They are not expecting to hear from you, and they're certainly busy when you call. So ask for no more time than you need for this first call: sixty seconds.)*

My company works closely with project managers of leading oil and gas firms, including Exxon and BP . . . *(Create a "flash of credibility" and relevance that communicates that to the prospect that you are someone who knows at least something about their business. This is also known in telesales vernacular as the "bandwagon" approach: since some of their competitors have already implemented your solution, you better hurry and jump on the bandwagon, too.)* . . . who are frustrated about the slow pace of project decision making. They're tired of the constant finger-pointing, excuses, and lack of accountability from subs. *(Notice that benefits are written in terms of customer problems.)*

We have a new project management collaboration tool that XYZ Company found speeds up project decision making by as much as 20 percent. *(Here's the result / benefit metric related to the project manager's number-one pain.)*

Do you have just a minute to hear a bit more? *(While the ultimate goal is to get the twenty-minute appointment, you want to ask for smaller commitments first. This is a test of your communication skills: in asking this question, you are anticipating that the prospect will need more information before they will agree to the twenty-minute appointment, but are curious enough to agree to "just a minute.")*

If you have done a good job, you're sure to hear something like:

PROSPECT: Tell me more. What is it?

JEANNETTE *(proceeds with another CPA round)*:

> *Courtesy:* Certainly.

> *Problem:* We have a new project management collaboration tool that enables any user, regardless of location or time zone, to both submit and obtain project information without going through expensive and time-consuming third-party service bureaus. Project managers are very frustrated because people always say they don't have updated project information.

> You can achieve "real-time" visibility into the project, which enables you to spot potential problems before they become costly delays. Each and every decision can be made 20 percent faster. And given all the decisions you make, 20 percent on every decision really adds up. *(Mix the shotgun problem statement up a bit so it doesn't sound the same. Also, I provided a little more specificity on my solution description. Again, specificity builds the prospect's interest.)*

> *Action:* The purpose of my call is to schedule a brief, twenty-minute appointment to introduce our new idea to you and get your professional opinion on it. Would you be available next Tuesday at 3:45? *(I had Jeannette clearly state her purpose: to obtain a twenty-minute appointment. That's it. Remember, the biggest mistake salespeople make here is they start selling the product/service. No. You are simply selling a twenty-minute appointment. "Get your professional opinion" suggests he/she is a professional, and that no high-pressure selling will occur. Change to "executive opinion" if you are calling an executive.)*

Tip: More Advice on Call Preparation

Before you pick up the phone, think about the following:

1. What do I know about this prospect?
2. Do I have two or three names of other companies that are either a) competitors or b) located nearby that I can name-drop?
3. What information can I or should I get from people other than the decision maker?
4. What is my opening, and is the problem statement strong enough to interest this prospect?
5. What specific questions will I ask?
6. What is my objective for this call? *(for the first call, it's to get the prospect to agree to a twenty-minute appointment)*
7. If I don't succeed at my number-one objective, what is my fallback position? *(such as setting a short appointment to talk again)*

Dealing with Objections and Obstacles

When you first ask for an appointment, be prepared to get an objection. Objections can also be handled using CPA. Here are some examples, using Jeannette's situation to illustrate a typical response.

The PROSPECT says, "Send me some literature."

JEANNETTE uses this as an opportunity to say:

> *Courtesy:* I certainly could, but it would take more time for you to read and review our literature than the twenty minutes it would take for us to meet and cover the highlights.

> *Problem:* Again, we have a new idea that can prevent costly project delays and prevent finger-pointing.

> *Action:* May I see you next Tuesday at 10:45?

The PROSPECT says, "You need to talk to our purchasing department."

JEANNETTE answers with the following:

> *Courtesy:* I'd be pleased to speak with purchasing.
> *Problem:* However, we offer a new strategy toward improved collaboration on project management teams that prevents costly delays. And strategy is your responsibility, not purchasing's.
> *Action:* Again, twenty minutes is all I ask, and then you can be the judge. Would next Wednesday afternoon work for you, perhaps 4:40? I'll be gone by 5 o'clock.

The PROSPECT says, "I'm just too busy right now."

JEANNETTE responds:

> *Courtesy:* I can appreciate that. But that's the very reason why you should take twenty minutes to meet with me.
> *Problem:* This new idea can prevent others from making excuses as to why they couldn't contribute to the project in a timely manner. And it's not only *your* time our tool saves, but *everyone else's* time who is working on the project.
> *Action:* Would Monday afternoon at 1:45 work, or would Thursday at 9:45 be better?

The PROSPECT says, "I'm not interested."

JEANNETTE:

> *Courtesy:* I understand. However, the purpose of my visit would not be to sell you anything that day.
> *Problem:* All I'm asking for is twenty minutes to introduce our new idea to you and get your professional opinion on it. If you like what you see then perhaps

you'll decide to try it out on a future project. We've helped some of the most successful oil and gas companies prevent delays caused by lack of real-time information.

➤ *Action:* If you can't spare twenty minutes, how about fifteen?

PROSPECT: We're happy with our present supplier.

JEANNETTE:

➤ *Courtesy:* I understand that your solution may be working for you at the moment . . .

➤ *Problem:* What I also know, however, is that needs can change very quickly,

➤ *Action:* Allow me to meet with you for twenty minutes and let me show you what we've got. Then, if your circumstances change in the future, you'll have some other options at hand.

Tip: Think High Persistence, Not High Pressure

In every situation other than a prospecting call, I recommend a selling process in which you act as a no-pressure consultant. However, calling busy executives for appointments can be difficult. Prospects are tougher over the phone because it's easy to reject a salesperson who isn't sitting in front of you.

So the salesperson needs to have a strong and focused approach. I think of it as developing "high persistence" rather than becoming "high pressure." Salespeople who lack persistence give up too quickly. They're gone after the prospect's first "no" response, and don't give themselves enough of a chance to use their approach skills.

Your ability to persist in the face of resistance, to refuse to give up, and to ask again for an appointment is a vital ingredient for a successful approach—and for sales success.

What to Do If You Get No Response to a Voice Mail

If you leave a voice mail message and don't receive a return phone call within a week, call again and leave the same message. If you still don't get a return call a week later, call a third time and leave the same message—with one minor, but significant difference:

"If now isn't the right time—or if you have no interest in meeting with me—let me know so I won't keep calling."

This important addition often gets an immediate reply. Sometimes the prospect will say, "Don't call me again." Other times you'll hear, "I'm sorry, I've just been busy, but if you'll call me this Friday afternoon I'll be able to talk with you." Any news is better than no news.

Have Some Fun!

I remember one day when I was a sales manager, I was doing a ride-along with Jack, one of my top salespeople. Jack had a downtown territory and we were between appointments. So Jack pulled out a list of fifty prospects and their phone numbers. Jack got a busy lawyer on the phone and started with our "spiel" about our "new idea." After giving a few objections and hearing Jack handle them effectively, the lawyer said "Jack, I'm not going to agree to meet with you unless you tell me exactly what your product is first."

Jack replied, "Well Mr. Prospect, that would require at least ten minutes."

The prospect replied, "I have ten minutes. Go ahead."

Jack said, "Great, Mr. Prospect. I'm right across the street. I'll see you in two minutes!"

We raced over to the prospect's office and when he came out to the lobby, he was laughing out loud. He loved it!

Tip: Use Appointment Letters to Open More Doors

A well-crafted appointment letter, followed up with a phone call, is an excellent method for approaching busy prospects.

- ➢ An appointment letter saves your prospects time because it tells them the value that you offer.
- ➢ If the value you describe sparks their interest, they will agree to meet with you.
- ➢ Perhaps most important, an appointment letter lets you tell an executive assistant who answers the phone, "Mr. Jones is expecting my call."

You can find example appointment letters by going to www.topline leadership.com/free_downloads.

Preparing for the First Appointment

When you have successfully scheduled an appointment, it's time to become a Student again because you want to be fully prepared for your twenty-minute meeting. Take time to gather even more information on your prospect's business and current challenges. As the saying goes, "Luck is what happens when preparation meets opportunity." You're about to attend a twenty-minute meeting with "opportunity," so you want to be fully prepared.

CHAPTER 5

The Doctor

Diagnose Small Problems, Define Big Needs

I n an initial meeting with a VP of sales to discuss potential sales
training, I began by establishing rapport, then asked him a few
questions. Before long, I'd learned that he had a team of salespeople who sell advertising space for 300 billboards. When I asked
about his current level of sales, he told me he was at only 70 percent
of quota—and he was *not* pleased. Bingo!

What do you suppose most salespeople would do at this point?
They'd present the sales training as a *cure* for low sales. And I must
admit, I was sorely tempted to follow the old-school sales axiom
"find a need and fill it." Had I done that, if I'd said "I can teach your
salespeople how to sell more," he would have certainly asked for a
price. Suppose I had told him a two-day customized program for his
team would be about $18,500. What do you think his reaction
would have been? "Seems a little high . . . I can't afford it . . . don't
need it . . . it's not in the budget."

When salespeople present their product or service too soon,
they actually *cause* price/value objections. So when you hear "I can't
afford it" or "it's not in the budget," your first reaction shouldn't

be to go back to your manager and see if you can lower your price. **Remember, the value of your solution is determined by the value to the customer of solving the problem.** In other words, until you know the value of solving the problem for the customer, you don't know the value of your solution. Rather than jumping into a presentation of your solution right up front, you need to learn how to **ask better questions** with a goal of determining the value of a solution.

Uncovering Needs to Establish the Value of Your Solution

This chapter discusses one of the most important skills you can develop: **learning how to help your prospects tell *you* the value of your products and services.** The questions you ask in your role as Doctor will help your prospects sell themselves. It isn't your product or service that creates buyer interest. It is *their* recognition of the value of making a change. Besides, prospects will never object to things they say themselves. It's hard for them to say no to a proposal that they themselves created by virtue of giving voice to their own problems.

The key test of your being a sales consultant is this: Does your customer know a lot more about their problem(s) after you leave than before you showed up?

Since the billboard sales call is based on one of my actual experiences, I know what really happened. I resisted the temptation to pitch my product. I just kept asking questions.

"Mr. Prospect, can you tell me what's causing your sales problem?" He said it was "low prospecting activity" (notice that my probing got him to better define his problem). I then asked, "Why aren't your salespeople prospecting more?" And he answered that they don't have the skills and lack the confidence to call on higher-level decision makers. After a few more questions, I asked him "How much is that costing you?" He thought for a minute, then said "Probably about a million dollars so far this year." Then I asked, "Suppose you could increase your salespeople's prospecting activity to an acceptable level, how much of that million dollars in increased revenue would go directly to bottom-line profits?" He told me it would be about 65 percent.

Put yourself in his shoes. *Now* how do you feel about investing $18,500 in training for a potential $650,000 in profit? It's peanuts, right? Do you think he told me, "Let me think it over" or "I can't afford that?" No way!

Tip: Why You Shouldn't Jump to Your Solution

As you can see from this example—and probably know from your own experience—starting to present your solution at the very first meeting with a contact has a number of problems:

> It shifts the focus away from the customer and on to you.

> At this point in the customer's buying process you don't really know the full value of your solution.

> You also don't know what problems or opportunities the customer has and does not have—so you may end up emphasizing features they don't want and missing capabilities they do want.

> It makes the customer feel like they are being "sold to" and makes you sound like every other salesperson who's been calling on them.

My approach was that of a **doctor** who helped the patient diagnose the cause of his own discontent. A doctor helps you achieve wellness through knowledge and questioning. Using lab tests, a physical exam, your medical history, and a description of your current symptoms, the doctor diagnoses your problem, helps you understand what other complications will occur, and then discusses what's necessary for a cure.

By assuming the role of a doctor and properly diagnosing seemingly little problems, you can uncover big needs that increase the value of your product or service in your customers' eyes! Slowing down in this step, taking the time for proper diagnosis, is one of the biggest levers you will have for speeding up your customer's buying process.

Customer Step 2: *Discontent*

At the *Discontent* step of the buy-learning process, prospects recognize a problem or an opportunity for improvement. In their minds, they question the seriousness of the problem and determine whether or not to take action, whether or not they have a need to buy.

Statements that indicate a prospect is in the *Discontent* step include:

> "I wish we could ..."
> "We can't ..."
> "It would be nice if ..."
> "How much? What's the ballpark cost?"

The last indicator, about ballpark cost, arises because the prospect recognizes there's a problem and wants to get some idea of what a solution would cost. Do not make the mistake of interpreting this question as a buying signal. The customer is at a crossroads: if it appears that the cost to buy a new solution is greater than the cost of the problem, the buying process likely comes to a halt; if the cost seems low compared to the impact of the problem, the buying process continues. (One of your goals in the Doctor role is therefore to help your prospects recognize the full scope of their problems so they can make the proper cost/benefit choice.)

During the *Discontent* step, a customer goes through the following phases:

1. **Recognizing a problem or opportunity:** *Discontent* occurs when prospects recognize that where they are now (their actual situation) is not where they would like to be (their optimal situation). *Discontent* can be caused by an awareness of either a *problem* or an *opportunity*. A problem relates to the past; some-

thing bad or unacceptable that has already occurred (delays, defects, rework, unhappy customers, etc.). An opportunity looks to the future, such as the potential of strengthening their market position, entering a new market to increase sales, etc.

When attempting to diagnose prospects' needs, many salespeople make the mistake of asking questions to uncover only *problems*; that is, they look exclusively at what has already happened. Salespeople who look only for problems are like drivers who look only in the rearview mirror. They are not focused on where their customers want to go. They should look for needs that originate from both problems *and* opportunities.

2. **Asking, "How serious is the problem?":** Prospects usually have numerous problems but limited resources for solving them. For this reason, when they see a need, they ask themselves: "How serious is it?" They prioritize their problems and allocate their resources accordingly. Prospects' *Discontent* can vary in intensity, depending on whether a small nuisance or a major crisis is perceived. The more serious the prospects' *Discontent*, the greater the value of the solution, and the more resources the prospects will make available to solve it.

3. **Asking, "How much will the solution cost?":** Prospects are very sensitive to price during the *Discontent* step. I'm sure you can recall a prospect asking you, early in a sales process, "Can you give me a rough estimate: *how much* is your solution?" By this time, prospects believe they understand the seriousness of their *Discontent* and want to put a dollar figure on the fix. Determine ahead of time how you'll handle this question (some hints are given later in this chapter).

4. **Determining "I need to buy!":** When prospects have taken ownership of the need, they see themselves as having bought your product/service or something similar to it. They form a mental image of its value, an expectation of the results that will occur as a consequence of buying. The greater your prospects' vision of value to be gained, the greater their desire to buy.

Tip: Be Alert for Inaccurate Perceptions of Needs

Customers in the *Discontent* step may think they have their problem well defined, but in my experience that is often not the case. For example, the executive of the billboard advertising company thought his salespeople had a problem with prospecting, but it turned out to be a problem with diagnostic questioning. Such inaccurate perceptions are, in part, why your role of Doctor is so critical to helping your customers get solutions that will truly generate the results they want to see.

As a sales consultant, your goal is to help the customer get the information they need to get through these phases without bogging them down. Putting on your Doctor hat and asking diagnostic questions will help both them and you unearth the information critical to making this buying decision. It is the first step in helping you and your prospect understand the extent of their needs/opportunities, and therefore what value a solution can deliver.

Types of "Patients" You Will Meet

Before prospects recognize the need to buy, they must feel dissatisfied with where they are now. Your focus early in a sales process should be to determine the gap between what is and what should be. It is within this gap that discontent resides.

A Doctor of sales deals with three kinds of patients, as shown in Figure 5-1:

- Sick patients: Those whose performance is below normal.
- Healthy patients: Those who are generally doing OK but who know they could be doing much better.
- "In denial" patients: Those who think they are healthy, but whose doctor knows that is not their true condition!

Figure 5-1 Types of Customer "Patients"

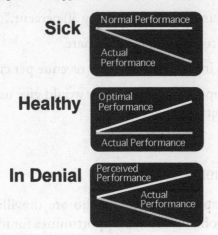

"Sick" Patients

These are prospects whose performance is not up to par at the moment. Usually, they function at an acceptable (or normal) level, but they perceive that lately their actual performance has been substandard and those issues need to be addressed.

Sick prospects will use statements that clearly indicate a problem of some sort:

> "Our costs are too high."
> "Defects and rework are killing us."
> "Our customers complain about _____."

"Healthy" Patients

The performance of healthy prospects may be at an acceptable level, but they seek the *opportunity* to be better off and to achieve a higher level of performance. This is the prospect that wants to go from good to great.

A prospect that is generally healthy but still has a need or opportunity that your solution can help address will say things like:

> "I want more customers."

> "Our goal is to increase sales by 30 percent."

> "We need to increase market share."

> "We must increase our average revenue per customer."

> "Greater operational efficiency would give us a huge leg up on our competitors."

"In Denial" Patients

In-denial prospects are people who are unwilling to talk about either their problems or their opportunities for improvement. They believe their performance is optimal, but they are mistaken. These are the most difficult prospects to sell to because they are unwilling to admit a need. You will hear in-denial prospects say:

> "Business is wonderful." (Despite reports to the contrary.)

> "We're hiring lots of people." (Many others recently quit.)

> "Business couldn't be better." (In reality, it's the worst it has ever been.)

Getting Prospects to Open Up

Early during a meeting with a new prospect it is not uncommon for your prospect to be reluctant to converse with you. The two of you have just met, and now you're asking questions about his or her problems. If you sense that your prospect is reluctant to open up and talk about their company's problems, change the tack of your questions. Don't focus your questions around problems (don't ask "what's not working in your business?"). Instead, ask about potential opportunities for improvement. Ask, "Where do you think your organization can improve? As well as they are doing now, what do you feel they can do better?" If they won't open up then, either, it's time to move on to another sales opportunity.

Candidly, these are prospects you should get rid of. Don't waste your precious time on them, as you will get nowhere.

How the Doctor Intensifies the Prospect's Need for Change

One of the biggest differences between the buying-focused sales approach I use and approaches you might learn elsewhere is our focus on getting the prospects to recognize not just the *need* to change but the *value to them* of making a change. Good "Doctor" questioning will therefore help Sick or Healthy prospects identify that gap between where they are now and where they *should* be (or want to be). Exposing these gaps is what will help shift your clients from an awareness of the possibility of change to an actual desire to change.

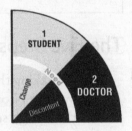

Many salespeople think they're consultative because they ask needs-based questions and listen to the answers before presenting their solution. This, however, is "expert selling," not "consultative selling." An expert tells someone else what to think. A consultant—or at least, a *good* consultant—helps the other person see their own situation in a new way and discover something that they don't already know.

When you "consult" with customers, *they* seek out *your* analysis, opinion, and expertise. The expertise that matters most is your knowledge of their business, their processes, and how your product or service can improve those processes. **A sales consultant understands that their most dangerous competitor at this stage is the customer's decision to do nothing.** (You're not really going up against your competition until the customer is in the *Comparison* step.) The most effective approach, therefore, is to use expert questioning—much as a doctor would do—to raise the priority of solving the problem by helping the customer better understand the impact of *not* changing.

Tip: Go In "Naked" TIP

In my seminars I advise salespeople to go into the first meeting "naked"—meaning you don't take in any literature or samples. If you introduce the topic of your company's products or services, you are essentially offering the customer a solution. And in doing so, you have moved past the customer, transitioning into the Learn phase while they are still in the Need phase. By offering a solution so early in the customer's buying process, you have also forfeited your #1 reason for meeting with other decision makers: to learn more about their needs. So slow down, go in naked, and keep focused on identifying your customer's needs.

The Five Steps of Diagnosis

When making that first twenty-minute sales call—whether in person or over the phone—you need to have a plan for leading your "patient" through self-discovery so they will convince themselves that it is a priority to solve their problems *now* (ideally, in the way you prescribe). Here are the five steps I use.

Step #1: Break the Ice Quickly

Your first objective is to establish credibility within the first two minutes of your meeting. The best way to do that is to tell prospects what you already know about their business because you were a good Student. Naturally, you'd want to do some brief introductions (if you are meeting with people you haven't talked to before) or other ice breaker, but quickly get to the purpose of the meeting:

"Thank you for agreeing to spend twenty minutes with me. I know your time is limited, so I'll just get started if I may. *(This indicates you will be conscious of their time and helps build your credibility with a busy executive.)* Are you familiar with _____ [name of your company]?" *(If necessary, give a sixty-second, elevator-speech type of description. Show the prospect a list of your clients or users of your products/service. This is a quick way to establish credibility.)*

(Now you want to bridge into asking them questions. Remember, you're not here to pitch your product. You want to learn about their needs and opportunities.) "Frankly, I'm not sure if what we offer can benefit your company, so I'd like to ask you some questions. Will that be OK?"

Step #2: Establish the Big Picture

Always start with a few big picture questions:

> "What is your number one goal?"
> "What obstacles will you need to overcome to achieve that goal?"
> "Any ideas on how you can overcome those obstacles?"

These questions help you determine which issues are dominant on your prospect's mind at that particular moment. Often, you will be able to link the problems and needs you discuss next with the customer to these big picture issues—which helps create greater momentum to buy.

Step #3: Ask Diagnostic Questions

There are some parallels between the diagnostic steps a doctor of medicine and a Doctor of selling will go through. When you go to a doctor's office, what's the first thing that happens once you're called into the exam room? Someone takes your vital signs. Then the doctor compares your current health with what your records show (your history), and ask if there are any problems you want addressed or improvements you want to make. As a Doctor of sales, you need to do the same thing: establish where your prospect is now, where they have been, and where they want to be.

There are five types of questions you should ask:

History Questions. Get background facts and current information. Identify actual performance and the ideal level of performance that the customer would like to achieve. You want to identify the difference between *what is* and *what should be*. History questions may also verify what you already know or suspect. For example:

- What are the changes going on in your business?
- What are your customers' expectations?
- Where are you now in relation to your company's goals?

Symptom Questions. After a doctor has established your baseline vital signs, the next question is often "what hurts?" For salespeople, the issue is why the prospect is dissatisfied, the source of their discontent. Typical symptom questions vary depending on whether you're dealing with a sick or healthy prospect:

- **Problem-Focused Questions** (when selling to a sick patient):
  - What kinds of problems are you experiencing?
  - Are you satisfied with _____?
  - Other customers have had difficulty with _____. Has this been a problem for you as well?
  - If there was one thing you could do to improve _____, what would it be?

- **Opportunity-Focused Questions** (when selling to a generally healthy patient):
  - What barriers stand between you and your goals?
  - Is your current level of performance acceptable to you?
  - What would you like to see improved?

Cause Questions. Prospects may or may not know the cause of their discontent. *Cause questions* will determine the source of the problems. If you don't find the cause of a problem, your solution won't resolve it. You can determine cause by asking:

- What do you attribute that to?
- Any idea what's causing that?
- What factors bring about that problem?

Experts trained in exposing the root causes of problems know that you have to dig deep. A standard practice they use is known as the "Five Whys" method. Someone mentions a problem and you ask them to explain *why* they think it happens. They give an answer, and you again ask *why* they think that next level of problem occurs, and so on until you reach what you believe is the root cause of the problem. (The number "five" here is not written in stone. It's just a reminder that you sometimes have to dig deep to expose root causes. Sometimes, you'll hit the root at Why #2; other times it may take more than five whys.)

For example, suppose a prospect said to a company that sells software for integrating payments, "Customers are frustrated with our billing system." The company representative would probe down the levels of "why":

WHY #1: "Why are customers frustrated?"

ANSWER: They complain about incorrect invoices, and overcharges, and the resulting late payment fees."

WHY #2: "Why are the invoices incorrect?

ANSWER: "Because prior payments aren't always entered correctly in the system."

WHY #3: "Why aren't payments entered correctly?"

ANSWER: "Sometimes they pay online and sometimes they mail in a check. Those are entered into our accounting software in different ways, and an invoice may go out before all the payments are entered."

Complication Questions. Prospects may also not realize the seriousness of their problem, which is important in helping them determine whether or not they have a pressing need. Complication questions get prospects to discuss the ripple effects of the problem—what will happen if they decide to do nothing. A goal of the Doctor role is helping patients recognize both the immediate and long-term consequences and costs associated with these complications.

Now is the time to apply the knowledge you gained as a Student and to help your prospects recognize the need for your offering. If you study your prospects' businesses in advance, you will be able to ask potent, targeted complication questions. By digging further to expose complications, you can reveal any big needs the prospect may be unaware of. Here are some examples of useful, open-ended complication questions:

> How does that affect _____?

> Does that lead to any other difficulties?

> What could happen if you don't solve that problem?

> What other problems does that create for you?

> That must cause real problems . . . (*then pause and allow the prospect to elaborate on the related difficulties*)

In practice, I compile a list of complications as I talk to a prospect, and then go back through the list one by one and ask, "How does this complication impact your business? What is it costing you?" (Secretly you're hoping the prospect doesn't know the answers to some of these questions because that gives you the perfect opening to get referred to another decision maker, when you ask, "Who *would* know the answer to this question?")

Cure Questions. These help you identify a prospect's expectations of value, their mental picture of desired results. The difference between complication questions and cure questions is important. Complication questions ask prospects to speculate on the negative effects and costs of a problem, developing the prospect's awareness of potential loss if nothing is done about the problem(s). Cure questions ask prospects to speculate on the potential value of a solution, highlighting what the customer will experience if they take action. Examples of cure questions are:

> If you were able to solve _____, what else would that enable you to do?

> How would that help?
> What other advantages would solving this problem have?
> How much do you think you'd save if you solved this problem?

Tip: What's More Important, the Question or the Answer?

Don't bend over backwards trying to ask the perfect question. Focus instead on what you want to learn: a prospect's symptoms, causes, and complications. If you think about the types of answers you are seeking, you will ask the right questions. Don't complicate the simplicity of this sales role.

Here's a real-life example to illustrate how this flow of questioning works: Marshall sells industrial flooring. He met with a prospect who wanted to patch a few divots left in his factory floor by a forklift. But Marshall saw a more serious problem. It was an old concrete floor, rapidly deteriorating from spilled acids and chemicals. His diagnostic questioning is captured in Table 5-1.

Note that complication questions also put you into a stronger position when your prospect moves into the *Research* and *Comparison* steps—covered in the next two chapters—because you'll be able to anticipate criteria that will be important to them and know just *how* important those criteria are.

Also notice that Marshall never *tells his prospect* what these complications are. He asks his prospect to *tell him*. As a salesperson, you can offer your insights, but you'll be more effective if you ask your prospects to speculate on the possible complications. This way they'll take ownership of the problem and be more committed to change. A simple truth is this: Prospects don't object to what they say themselves. When they articulate the potential crisis, it's their idea, not yours.

Through this questioning, Marshall was able to help the factory owner recognize that the floor condition was worse than he originally

Table 5-1 Example of Diagnostic Questioning

	MARSHALL'S QUESTIONS	CUSTOMER'S ANSWERS
History	When did you install your current floor? What types of chemicals have you been using in your factory? Do you know what types of chemical resistance products, if any, were included in the concrete?	The existing floor was eight years old, several hazardous materials were being used in the manufacturing process, and the prospect was unsure what types of components had gone into the original concrete mixture.
Symptom	Besides the divots, are you satisfied with the current condition of your factory floor?	The prospect told Marshall that the floor seemed to be holding up okay, although in a few areas the concrete had begun to break down. These areas were becoming increasingly difficult to clean.
Cause	What is causing the breakdown of the concrete?	Marshall learned about various types of spills that occurred during the manufacturing process. He also learned that the company's cleaning contractors were not effectively cleaning up these spills.
	. . . Why?	The prospect told him that because the texture of the floor was very rough, spills weren't easily wiped clean. Marshall also learned that some spaces between the concrete slabs were damaged, possibly enabling small amounts of hazardous chemicals to leak into the ground. Gradually this combination of factors was causing the floor to deteriorate.
Complication	If you had a serious spill, what might happen? Might that create some health or safety concerns? How do hazardous spills affect your insurance?	The manager soon recognized what might result if the floor wasn't replaced. There were some potential worker safety issues, potential liability for workman's compensation claims, environmental issues, possible legal fees—and certainly the possibility of negative publicity. So now, in the prospect's mind, his modest dissatisfaction with the condition of his factory floor has become a much more significant and tangible problem.
Cure	What other advantages would solving this problem have?	The prospect suddenly recognized an important benefit. Replacing the current "rough-textured" floor with a smoother surface would make it easier for the maintenance people to clean up spills.

thought. As a result, he sold a new, $50,000 acid-resistant floor—despite a competitor's $40K bid. Marshall's company uses higher-quality materials and has a better track record. Because the customer felt the purchase was of such major importance, the manufacturing manager was able to justify the added cost of Marshall's solution.

Tip: An Additional Cure Question

To conclude diagnostic questioning, ask, "In comparison to your other issues and challenges, how important a priority would this issue be?" Asking your customer to reflect on the importance of this issue compared to others will give you an indication of how motivated they will be to resolve it.

Step #4: Determine the Complex Buying Team

As I discussed in Chapter 3, ultimately, you need to answer four sets of questions when you're dealing with a Complex Buying Team:

> Who will be involved in the decision? Where are they at in their buying process?

> Who are the most influential decision makers? At what stages of the buying process will they be involved?

> What does each decision maker want? What are their needs?

> What is the attitude of the most influential decision makers about your company and its solution?

You won't be able to answer all of these sets of questions at the very first meeting with your contact, but you should begin laying the groundwork by at least asking *how* the decision will be made. And as you go through the rest of the process with your customer, think carefully about how you will answer the remaining questions.

Use 3×3 Prospecting. For important account opportunities, strive for relationships with a minimum of three different people, preferably at three different levels. A relationship based on a single contact at an account is risky. You'll get better information from all contacts if each of them knows you have other relationships established within their business. Once you've identified the members of the Complex Buying Team, your goal should be to talk to as many of those decision makers as you can.

Remember the strategy recommended in Chapter 3, about going down the corporate ladder before going up it? I suggested that a first meeting with a Super User be followed by a second appointment with a lower-level User (to observe the "need in action"), and a third appointment with the Super User and the COO (the ROI Authority). Three people at three levels: that's 3×3 prospecting.

Step #5: Offer the Minimum Prescription

Once your prospects recognize a need to solve a problem, they will be immediately curious about your solution. Now, you must demonstrate that you can help them to accomplish their stated goals. Your prospects must know that a solution is feasible, otherwise there is no reason to proceed to the next buying step (*Research*).

The bottom line is this: Don't start talking in specifics about your solution! Remain focused on the customer's needs throughout the first meeting and work your way into the logical position that there may be some doubts about the customer's needs. That's your justification for getting closer to the customer's issues and concerns. Once you gather that knowledge, guess what—that's the exact information that the C-level ROI Authority is interested in: understanding the issues. If you can develop a new perspective on the issues that created the customer's need, use that insight as a bargaining chip to share your findings with the ROI Authority.

If the prospect presses you about your solution, respond in generalities. When pressed, you can respond with a client success story, but end the story with, "That was their need, and I'm not sure it's yours. Allow me to do a bit more investigating *[with some other expert back at your office]* and then I'd like to meet with you and your decision-making team to share my analysis."

Just as a doctor prescribes no more medication than necessary, so too should a Doctor of selling present only those capabilities that achieve the specific result(s) that prospects desire. The results your prospects expect are revealed to you in the answers to your cure questions. By presenting the capabilities you can offer to achieve the desired results, you are showing your prospects that you listened.

The purpose of your prescription is not to outline a total treatment plan. It's too soon for that. You just want your customers to get enough of an answer that they will continue on to Step 3, *Research*.

Handling the "Ballpark Price" Question

It's natural for customers to ask for a ballpark price sometime in the first or second meeting. However, this is a tricky question for salespeople. As you now know, few customers have a solid grasp on the exact extent or nature of their problem or opportunity, or on what an optimal solution will look like. If you toss out a dollar figure now, the customer will be hooked onto that figure, even if the scope or nature of the solution changes in later steps of their buying process.

So what can you do? One option is to acknowledge the customer's interest in getting an answer to the question, but then asking to delay giving an answer: "Please allow me to ask more questions so I can understand your needs better. Then I'll analyze what I learn and put a figure down on paper." (Note you don't commit to exactly *when* that number will get written down.)

Another option is simply to give a very wide range of potential costs. If you do decide to mention your price at this point, watch the prospect's facial features very carefully for the telltale signs of surprise. According to research conducted by Dr. Paul Ekman, author of *Unmasking the Face: A Guide to Recognizing Emotions from Facial Clues*, true surprise in your prospects can be detected visually.[10] You have to pay close attention to your prospect's facial features, because surprise is the briefest of emotions; it only lasts a fraction of a second. And if it lasts longer, it's likely a bluff.

Practice detecting surprise by saying something surprising to a friend or loved one and watch for the clues. Then, ask the person to feign the appearance of surprise and you'll notice the difference. Better yet, buy Ekman's book.

Identify then Intensify *Discontent*

Selling is the process of uncovering urgency, and defining it in the mind of your customer. The more momentum you generate early on in the process, the greater the probability that you'll make a sale.

In your Doctor role, your goal is to identify your prospects' degree of discontent, then intensify that discontent with urgent questions so your prospects become more motivated to continue with the buying decision.

Again, the key test of your being a sales consultant is this: Does your customer know a lot more about their problem(s) after you leave than before you showed up?

MILESTONE #2

Accelerating Momentum with a Memo of Understanding (MOU)

Way to go! You just completed a successful initial meeting with a new prospect. Your prospect now has a clearer picture of the nature and extent of their Need and a more urgent desire to seek a solution. You have two challenges now, however. The first is inherent unreliability of memory (especially in this day and age when people have so much going on). The second is that the person you just met with cannot make this buying decision alone. So if you are to succeed (eventually) in making the sale, the person you met with must now go and sell other decision makers on the idea that an explicit Need exists that should be examined.

For both reasons, it pays to put down what you've just talked about with your contact in writing in an **MOU (Memo of Understanding).** An MOU is a short email you send after the initial appointment that **confirms key points** discussed during your meeting with the prospect: **the customer's current situation, critical issues,** and **complications**. At the end of the MOU you want to reconfirm the customer's go-forward commitment, the specific action the prospect told you he or she would take, along with a deadline by which it will be completed.

Why MOUs Are Critical

Of all the tools that I share with the salespeople, the single tool I consider most important is the MOU, hands down.

I'm a firm believer in MOUs because they work. Salespeople tell me that just knowing they'll be writing an MOU after a meeting causes them to ask *more* questions—and *better* questions—during the meeting. So MOUs help you to slow down your selling process, which helps you sell faster and sell more.

One of the largest sales I ever made happened because I sent an MOU to a regional sales manager of a very large national company immediately after our initial meeting. I succinctly described, based on the conversation he and I had, his company's symptoms, causes, and complications. The regional sales manager was an influential individual within his company. He forwarded my memo to his boss along with a suggestion to "take a look at this." His boss, who was in charge of sales for the whole eastern seaboard, forwarded the memo to the VP of sales for the entire company, who then forwarded it to the corporate director of training.

About two months after I sent the MOU to the regional sales director I received a call from the training director. That's when the *Research* and *Comparison* steps of the buying process occurred. Several weeks later I was successful in selling a "pilot" program, an initial sales training workshop for the client to try out our program with a select group of their company's top salespeople.

When I eventually delivered the first workshop, the training director was sitting in the back row. As I was discussing the value of MOUs with a group of his salespeople, he suddenly raised his hand and announced to the participants, "I've got the MOU Kevin sent to our company six months ago right here in my inbox. What he's saying is true. The MOU is the reason he's here." On the next break we hooked up his computer to the LCD projector and he displayed to everyone the trail my MOU email had taken prior to arriving in his inbox. Each executive who had received it had made comments, then forwarded it on. My MOU had acted like a pinball.

Obviously, not all of the MOUs that you send will be forwarded from one decision maker to another, even though you'd like that to happen. However, under no circumstances should *you* forward it to other people *without the explicit approval from your prospect!* The MOU you send to your prospect is a confirmation of a private conversation. He or she will not want what they said to you communicated to others within their company without their approval.

MOUs serve another important purpose. If you've made a good impression on your contact, *their* next step will be to raise the issue with other decision makers. So who is the salesperson now? That's right. Your contact—who, you hope, is becoming your Sponsor. And he or she hasn't yet read this book. So they're likely to sell too fast, too. Specifically, your Sponsor is entering the *Research* step, but must go and persuade other decision makers who are in the *Change* or *Discontent* steps to recognize a Need. For your contact, the MOU provides a convenient synopsis *of their own thinking* that can help them talk succinctly and knowledgeably about the problems, causes, and complications to the other decision makers they need to approach.

MOUs are first used early in the buying process, but you can also use them later when you know you have a strong Sponsor, someone who wants you and your solution to succeed, and you want to provide them with language they can use to sell you internally

If your first meeting with the prospect occurs later in the buying process, such as in the *Comparison* step, the MOU is much less effective. It's OK to send the MOU in other situations—just don't expect as much.

And at the very least, the MOU you send after the first appointment is an excellent place to start your *second* meeting with a prospect. Begin with a quick review of the MOU before transitioning into the Architect role, where the focus shifts to designing a solution. (Also, many salespeople I've worked with tell me that MOUs differentiate them from the competition. So that's a benefit, too. Most salespeople just won't take the time.)

Sample MOU

A good MOU is short, written in the customer's terms (not your company jargon). It clearly defines the customer's problems or opportunities, and the *impact* those issues will have if addressed or if not addressed. Also, it includes a go-forward commitment (see pages 53–55), the specific next-step action that your prospect agreed to take at the end of your first meeting. The sample MOU that follows illustrates each of these elements.

Sample Memo of Understanding

FROM: Alex@slowdown.com
TO: David@customer.com
SUBJECT: Recap of our conversation

Hi David -
Thanks so much for organizing our discussion today! I thought it would be a good idea to review the main points from our call to ensure we are on the same page.

Current Situation
• Screening about 700 applicants a year
• Not currently testing at all
• Average cost of a bad hire is around $10,000

Opportunities for Improvement
• Suffering higher turnover than you would like, typically within 90 days of hire, currently costing your company about $150,000/year
• Some hires not able to retain what is taught during training, which reduces the effectiveness of your training investment
• Some candidates are simply not a good job fit

Components of a Potential Solution
• You would like to find a predictive tool that assesses the actual on-the-job skills
• You need to refine and streamline your selection process
• You may want to pre-screen candidates that apply online
• You would like to plan a 90-day pilot to assess whether or not a tool is selecting a better quality of candidate

Are these issues accurate? I'll look forward to meeting with you again next Tuesday at 3 PM to review your invoices from your current provider. Please feel free to call or email me with any questions that come up!

Thanks again,
Alex
Account Executive

CHAPTER 6

The Architect

Design Customer-Focused Solutions

Early in my career I stopped by the radiology department of a medium-sized hospital. From the receptionist, I learned that the department was using outdated dictation equipment. A few days later, I sent the chairperson of the department an appointment letter. After several attempts to reach him by phone, I was finally successful in speaking with him and scheduling an appointment.

Having been trained in a traditional four-step sales approach (Approach / Needs / Present / Close), I began the sales call with comfortable conversation, which was successful in building trust. I then began questioning my prospect about his needs. During this portion of the call, I helped him recognize a serious problem with his current equipment. The solution—new dictation equipment— would enable his department to become much more productive. Gradually, over the next fifteen or twenty minutes, he recognized the need for new equipment. Next, as I had been taught, I began to present my high-end product, emphasizing its most popular features and benefits.

What I know now—but didn't know then—is that once my prospect recognized a need, he had moved forward in his buying process from Step 2, *Discontent,* to Step 3, *Research.* His focus had changed from *"Should* I buy?" to *"What* should I buy?" He began learning, in an effort to identify the capabilities necessary for a solution. As I was presenting my product, my prospect was thinking, "Hmmm, which of these capabilities do I need? No, not feature A. Feature B looks interesting, but I'm not sure I would use it. Oooh, feature C would be nice. And, yep, I've got to have that feature D."

When I reached the end of my presentation, I asked for the order. My prospect told me he needed some time. He said he would check his budget figures later in the week, and asked me to call him the following Monday. When I left my prospect's office, I knew he was interested, but I had no idea which capabilities he considered most important. I had done a good job helping him to recognize a need for new dictation equipment, but I had not worked with him to refine his needs. That day, I made the mistake I've been cautioning you against: I had not joined him in his buying process. I had seen the sale through my eyes, not his.

I did follow up as he requested, but had trouble getting through. Eventually I learned from his assistant that he had bought a system from one of my competitors that had fewer bells and whistles.

The kind of dictation equipment I was selling back then has gone the way of the dinosaur. But I still see this exact sales situation happening all too often—largely as a result of the underlying disconnect between a salesperson's selling process and a customer's buying process. Yes, I know you think that surely by the time the customer has made a decision to buy *something,* you should be able to talk about your product. Hold off a little bit longer. This is another critical point where slowing down will help you sell faster.

Management guru Peter Drucker once said, "The best way to predict the future is to create it." This chapter is about how you can become an Architect who can shape a differentiated solution that meets your customer's needs.

Orienting on the Buying Process

As a Student, you studied the changes affecting your prospects. As a Doctor, you diagnosed your prospects' discontent and uncovered important needs. Now, you're at the point of the sales process where prospects think "I know I need to buy something, but I'm not sure what to buy." So they begin a learning process to ensure they select the solution that best meets their needs. This learning process occurs during the third and fourth steps of the buying process: *Research* (covered in this chapter) and *Comparison* (discussed in the next chapter).

If your buyers are concerned about the possibility of making a mistake (and they almost always are), they will take rational action to ensure that they make the best choice by investigating what it will take to fulfill the needs they identify.

Your primary objective when customers are in the *Research* step of the buying process is to clarify their vision of a solution and create a blueprint for achieving that vision. To do that, you have to become a sales Architect who can design a solution the customer will be happy with, and influence their buying criteria in a way that best meets their needs while simultaneously creating a competitive advantage for you. A secondary objective is to make sure your prospects don't turn around and buy your competitors' products or services.

Customer Step 3: *Research*

Tim was interested in buying a security system for his home, so he scheduled appointments with three vendors.

The first two vendors presented Tim with their standard pitch for a four-bedroom/two-bath configuration, and each quoted a price during the meeting. Tim found himself asking a lot of product and price-oriented questions to learn more about security systems. Both of these vendors pitched Tim on why their company's service was the best choice.

When the third vendor arrived, Tim started the appointment by asking the same kinds of product and price-oriented questions he had asked the first two vendors. However, this salesperson said he needed to ask Tim a few questions about *his* needs before making any recommendations. The very first question he asked Tim really made an impact: "What are you trying to protect—people or stuff?"

This question caused Tim to stop and consider his primary goal for his new security system—what he was specifically trying to accomplish.

Tim realized his primary purpose was to safeguard his wife and children. Protecting personal property was, at least in comparison to his family's safety, a relatively insignificant concern. Therefore, from Tim's perspective, safety was a "must-have" requirement in a security system, while prevention of theft was merely a "nice-to-have" capability.

For the next half-hour, the customer-focused salesperson continued asking Tim questions about his needs. Then he pulled out a piece of paper and began designing Tim's home security system, emphasizing the components that affect the safety and security of the inhabitants—such as motion sensors and other deterrents. As he did so, Tim was thinking to himself, "Finally, a salesperson who's interested in helping *me* achieve *my* goals."

Salesperson #3 was fulfilling the role of an Architect, using a solution-design approach. Though his proposal was 15 percent higher than the other two, Tim had so much confidence in this salesperson and the solution design that he agreed to the additional investment.

Why was Tim willing to spend more on the third salesperson's solution? Because the first two salespeople had sold too fast. They thought that since Tim had called them in and expressed interest in having a security system that he would be persuaded by their company's superior product and service. The third salesperson, in contrast, took the time to understand Tim's mental picture of a solution, and then help frame a much more vivid picture. Salesperson #3 made Tim think.

If you're still pushing your own sales process like the first two salespeople who met with Tim, you'd better hope that there isn't anyone like Salesperson #3 in the picture. Even better, adopt the role

Tip: Why It's Still Important to *Not* Pitch Your Solution

As I've emphasized throughout the Student and Doctor roles, it's important that you *not* jump into talking about all the selling points of your product or service. But the urge to jump ahead is so tempting that I want to emphasize again that it's still too soon to begin "the pitch." Until you have helped the customer frame an effective solution for their needs or opportunities, you don't know what to emphasize about your product or service. If you can resist the temptation to talk about your product—and instead, keep the conversation focused on your customer's needs—then customers will think you're the best salesperson they've ever worked with.

of an Architect like Salesperson #3 and, if your competition is like the first two salespeople in this story, you'll still have the edge even if the customer has already met with your competition.

The Customer's Process for Developing a Solution

As the customer transitions out of the Need phase of buying and into the Learn phase, they begin by doing *Research*. They will:

> Talk about what their solution must or should do.

> Ask questions about your solution's capabilities.

What you have to remember is that the customer is only at the *beginning* of their learning process. They are looking for information that is going to help them make a better buying decision. They will begin to define standards or criteria by which they judge the relative value of available solutions—and a single buying criterion can make or break the choice between alternatives. Remember, it's not what's important to us, it's what's important *to the buyer*.

Consider, for example, two cars that are identical except one has a luggage rack and the other doesn't. Clearly, the luggage rack is a difference between the two vehicles, *but it is only a buying criterion if it is important to the buyer.* If the customer doesn't care about a luggage rack, then it isn't a criterion. Salespeople who spend too much time talking about a capability before finding out if the customer needs it will hinder their sales process. The customer will grow impatient and perhaps wonder, "Why pay for features I don't need?"

Customers in the *Research* step are just formulating their mental image of a solution, not yet comparing specific products or services. They are thinking, "What will fix my problem?" You can help them through this process by first having in your own mind a clear understanding of how your company and your solution are different from your competitors. Your differentiators enable your solution to solve customer problems in a different and hopefully better way than your competitors' solutions. Knowing this will help you raise these issues/problems with customers so *they* will recognize the importance of selecting a solution that will solve those problems. Don't talk about your product. Instead, keep the conversation focused on customer problems.

In other words, you want to help **shape your customer's buying criteria to include the unique strengths of your product or service.** That way, when they shop around later in the buying process, they'll recognize that certain factors they now consider important are the real strengths of your offering. In essence, you are designing a solution that not only does a good job of meeting customer needs but also sets the ground rules in your favor. **You want to answer the customer's question, "Why should we buy from you?" before *they ask it.*** And your answer should include specific reasons that are important to your customer because they're connected to the customer's needs.

Understanding Customer Buying Criteria

A buying criterion is a difference between alternative solutions, a difference that the buyer considers important. Your customers are going to base their buying decision on a number of criteria. But not all of those criteria are created equal. There will be **must-have** criteria that are absolutely essential and **nice-to-have** criteria that define other options the customer would like. If all proposed solutions meet the must-have criteria, customers will then move onto comparing nice-to-have criteria.

For the sake of demonstration, let's use a simple example. Suppose you're a commercial building contractor who needs a dump truck to move dirt from the loading site to your construction sites. (I use a dump truck example because it's likely that most readers will know as much about dump trucks as your customers know about your product or service!)

Your must-have criteria are factors that relate to what the vehicle must be able to do for you. It's got to hold dirt, move dirt, and dump dirt. Each criterion is necessary for solving the problem, and each allows you to eliminate virtually hundreds of vehicles from consideration. In this way, you can divide all the alternatives into those that are acceptable and those that are unacceptable.

Now suppose you have identified two vehicles that meet your must-have requirements: they hold dirt, move dirt, dump dirt. One option is a dual-axle dump truck with a larger payload. Let's call this Solution A. The other is a smaller, single-axle dump truck (Solution B). Since both meet the must-haves, what other factors can differentiate the two solutions under consideration? Table 6-1 shows four nice-to-haves and how the two solutions compare.

Which truck you decide to buy depends on which nice-to-have differences are identified and how *you* prioritize those differences. For example, you'd go with Solution B if purchase price is more important to you than speed of completion, labor costs, and maintenance costs.

Suppose your contract to move the dirt contains a severe penalty clause if the work isn't done on time. Under this scenario, your preference would be Solution A because your nice-to-haves would be ranked differently. The truck's capacity, which directly impacts on time to completion, would be of primary importance. Still important, but less so, would be labor costs, purchase price, and maintenance costs.

Table 6-1 Comparison of Nice-to-Have Criteria

CRITERIA	SOLUTION A (MAC TRUCK)	SOLUTION B (CHEVY)	ADVANTAGE
Price	$70K	$35K	B
Time to complete jobs	Bigger capacity; fewer trips needed	Smaller capacity; more trips needed	A
Labor costs	Less time needed	More time needed	A
Maintenance costs	Lower	Higher	A

The Dynamics of Customer Buying Criteria

You'll be in a strong starting point if you identify a customer's must-have and nice-to-have criteria, but don't think you can do this just one time and be done with it. Why?

The criteria will likely evolve as they go through the buying process. Customers learn much more about their needs and how those needs can be addressed as they go through each step of the buying process. You should check with your customer frequently to see if they have added new criteria, shifted the importance of some criteria, or deleted some criteria previously identified.

The *buying* criteria may be only a subset of the *decision* criteria. I've found that the choice between potential suppliers often comes down to a handful of criteria, even if the customer identified twice or three times as many criteria for making the decision. Why? In the *Research* and *Comparison* steps, the customer may learn that a certain factor they considered important in your solution is also available from the competition. That criterion is still important in the decision, but it does not help them choose between you and your competitor, so it recedes into the background as a factor used in the final buying decision.

Customers will view your solution as ideal only if you do the best job of incorporating most if not all of their criteria, and your work reflects how their understanding and criteria have shifted over time. And that's why your best bet when a customer is in the *Research* step is to become an Architect.

How an Architect Designs Unique Solutions

Salespeople who have been passive during the needs analysis, relying on the customer's ability to diagnose their own needs, often try to adopt an expert role when the customer is in their *Research* and *Comparison* steps. These salespeople step in and start describing the solution *they* have developed, assuming the customer will see it as a perfect fit. I've seen very experienced salespeople ruin the best chance they have to build mega-credibility at the *beginning* of the customer's buying process by coming across as the "expert" and talking too quickly about their solution.

From now on, let your competitors make this mistake! Not you. Rarely does a need identified by the customer match exactly the strengths of your offering. We too often allow customers to diagnose their own needs, and then tell them all about our solution. It's better for us to diagnose, or at least confirm their diagnosis, before we join the customer in their *Research* and *Comparison* steps. It's like getting a second opinion from a doctor. The best approach is collaborative, more of a joint discussion than assuming the mindset of an expert.

In my sales seminars, I ask salespeople to pick one of their sales opportunities that's currently in the *Research* or *Comparison* phase of the decision—and make a list of that customer's buying criteria. Many salespeople have difficulty completing this task. Often, they find themselves guessing. Next, I ask them to identify the criteria of a customer who recently purchased from them. This time, the list they come up with is usually much longer. To me, this proves many

---

Tip: How to Handle "Show Me What You've Got" TIP

What do you do with a prospect who says "show me what you've got" the moment you walk in the door? This is a very direct prospect who may have already spent considerable time analyzing his or her own needs, either alone (at the Step 3, *Research* level) or with your competitor (at Step 4, *Comparison* level).

There are two ways to handle this situation. First, you can say, "I've got fourteen different services and each service has multiple options. It would be a waste of your time to show you something you don't need. If you'll allow me to ask a few questions first . . ." Or you can show your product or describe your service to satisfy the prospect's demanding curiosity, then immediately back up to identify the problem or opportunity the prospect is trying to solve.

Regardless of which technique you choose, you cannot make solution recommendations without knowing about the prospect's *Discontent* and *Research* steps. Otherwise, you'll be guilty of sales malpractice: prescribing the solution without fully understanding the needs.

---

salespeople aren't uncovering customer needs, as defined by their buying criteria, soon enough.

Identify Your Differentiators (Do a Market Assessment)

In your role as an Architect, your job is to create the best match possible between your offering and your prospects' must-haves and nice-to-haves. Before talking with customers about their criteria, it helps if you know how your product or service compares to what else is available on the market. I think of this as doing a **market assessment**:

Step 1: List typical must-have and nice-to-have criteria used by prospects when they are considering your product or service. These must be **from your customer's perspective** and **reflect the interests of each player on the Complex Buying Team.**

Step 2: Compare your offering to the market alternatives with regard to these issues. For each criterion, identify where you are average (the same as the overall market), or either moderately or significantly superior or inferior.

Table 6-2, for example, shows a market assessment by one company that sells eight-passenger corporate jets. (This is a sample only; a full-fledged market assessment will likely have more criteria than this, and will be customized to each typical decision maker, i.e., the CEO's criteria will be different from the jet pilot's criteria.)

When creating your own market assessment, be sure to include criteria where you know you have a differentiator.

The market assessment does *not* look at specific competitors. Instead it addresses the entire collection of market alternatives. At this phase of the sale, you do not yet know who your specific competitors may be. By comparing yourself to the marketplace in general, you:

Table 6-2 Market Assessment on an Eight-Passenger Corporate Jet

CRITERIA	RATING
Range	A
Cruising speed	SS
Takeoff distance	S
Cabin comfort	BA
Support capabilities	A
Price	S
Brand recognition	A
Jet engine manufacturer	S
Avionics	S

A = average
S/SS = superior/significantly superior
BA = below average
SBA = significantly below average

➤ Clarify your strengths (the differentiators that will help you make the sale).

➤ Know your vulnerabilities.

➤ Will be better prepared to listen for key words or issues the customer mentions that are linked to either a differentiator or vulnerability.

➤ Prepare for weaknesses and objections you will encounter as you try to shape a solution that best meets your customer's needs, both in this step and as you set a strategy for winning as a Coach (see the next chapter).

The Architect's Toolkit: How to Understand and Influence Buying Criteria

Just as Salesperson #3 in the story earlier in this chapter helped Tim better define what he wanted in a security system, your role as an Architect is to ask questions that help both you and your customer clarify the customer's mental picture of a solution. You want to help the customer make a better buying decision by **helping them develop better definitions of their criteria and/or by exposing them to additional buying criteria they may find important.** (And if those new criteria happen to be differentiators for your offering, so much the better.)

There are four tools that comprise what I call the Architect's Toolkit that you can use to help sharpen the customer's mental image:

1. Diagnostic probing (if needed).

2. Establishing the solution criteria.

3. Planting a seed.

4. Turning intangibles into tangibles; turning vague criteria into specifics.

Tool #1: Diagnostic Probing (If Needed)

If you have created a particular sales opportunity or have been with the buyer through Step 1, *Change,* and Step 2, *Discontent,* of the buy-learning process, you will already be familiar with the buyer's core issues—the problem they are trying to fix or opportunity they want to take advantage of. So you may not need to do any diagnostic probing at this point.

However, if this is the first opportunity you have to talk with a customer, ideally you want to ask the kind of diagnostic questions you normally would have asked in the Doctor role, such as, "Tell me about the issues and concerns that caused you to start looking at this buying decision." It's that in-depth information about their needs that is your secret weapon. Be aware, however, that they may not want to spend much time talking about their needs, viewing it as backtracking (because they have already moved on to designing a solution).

Tool #2: Establishing the Solution Criteria

Once you have an idea of the customer's general concept, you want to identify specific buying criteria that the solution will need to meet. Ask:

> What does the ideal solution look like to you?
> What factors will you consider most important in making your decision?
> What's the *next* most important factor? Next? *(Keep asking until they have no more answers.)*
> Which criteria *must* the solution meet? Which are nice-to-haves?

To shape an ideal solution, you need to know not only what is important to the client, but also why. One option is to weave in the "why" question as you elicit the criteria: "What's the most important factor? *Why* is it important? What will this factor help you accomplish?" Or you can wait until near the end of this process—after you've used all the tools in this toolkit to develop a more complete list of criteria—then ask the customer to discuss why particular criteria are important.

Keep in mind that it will be rare to have a customer whose initial list of buying criteria reflects all the major strengths of your product or service. However, you can plant a seed for additional criteria, as I'll discuss next.

Tool #3: Planting a Seed

This action is based on the possibility that your prior experience may have given you a better understanding of capabilities that will be useful to your current customer, an understanding better than this customer has themselves. That is, a customer may be placing lesser importance on criteria that you know reflect capabilities that they *will* find useful (and that your offering provides). The challenge is to get the customer to come to that realization on their own. And the way to do that is to plant a seed that gets them thinking about potential criteria they have not yet considered.

When customers begin to see the advantages you can bring to the table, they often refine their buying criteria to reflect those characteristics. To see if planting a seed could bear fruit for a customer:

1. Think about the market assessment you did and the unique differences your offering has compared to the competition.

2. List all the problems the prospects might experience in the future if they don't have your offering's particular capabilities.

3. Determine the questions you can ask your prospect to help them recognize the importance of those issues.

When influencing specifications, the basic idea is to point out to the prospect a problem that your product or service can solve. That means you don't talk about your product. Instead talk about the

---

Tip: Keep Focused on Customer Needs

In professional selling, you can lose credibility when you present a capability that the customer doesn't need. So the simple answer at this step of the buying process is to first *discuss the problems* your capability solves. If the customer is unconcerned about some types of problems, you can then adjust your sales process to focus on what *does* matter to them. The result is that you'll deliver a solution that better matches customer needs.

---

problems that the prospect will have if they lack a certain capability. This ensures that your dialogue is focused on the customer's needs and problems.

To plant a seed about other criteria that you think are important for a customer but that they haven't yet thought of themselves (and that you would like them to adopt as their own), ask something like:

> ➢ Other customers have told us that they have a problem with _____. Has this been an issue for you as well?
>
> ➢ Can you tell me more about what you see happening?
>
> ➢ Why do you think these problems are occurring?
>
> ➢ How has this affected your _____ [sales/effectiveness/operations, etc.]?

Tool #4: Turning Intangibles into Tangibles; Turning Vague Criteria into Specifics

There are many, many customer criteria that express intangible qualities about your product or service or that will be stated in only vague terms such as:

> ➢ Good service
> ➢ Durability

> Post-sales support
> Ease of use
> Comfort

Even something you might think of as tangible, such as cost, is intangible until it is defined in concrete terms. Is the customer viewing cost as "purchase price" or "lowest cost of operation"?

Both you and your prospect will be in a stronger position if you work to define intangible or vague criteria in more specific, concrete terms. From your standpoint, you need to know exactly what it is the customer is looking for and how they will be evaluating your solution. **You cannot make a case that some feature or capability of your product/service is tied to a customer need if you don't know how that need is defined.**

Equally important, pushing for specificity also ensures that different decision makers will be defining the criteria or requirement *in the same way*. Otherwise, you can get tripped up unless you learn that for one person, for example, "durability" means "time between failures" and for another, it means "time until replacement." Part of helping the customer learn is just this—helping the customer define intangibles in a single, tangible way.

To turn intangibles into tangibles, get the customer to define how they will evaluate whether a particular criterion will be met. Ask, for instance:

> What do you mean by _____?
> How will you measure that?

Going back to the dump truck example, it might be that "reliability" is on the must-have or nice-to-have list of criteria. The salesperson would then want to ask the potential buyer what they mean by reliability (with a likely answer along the lines of "starts every time" and/or "doesn't break down often"). If the truck you're selling does better based on data on frequency of repairs, then you have another criterion on which you can build a strong case.

Another option is to have the customer rethink the criterion by

Tip: Confirm the "Tangible" Definitions, Too!

One of the dangers at this point in the sales process is that you will have terms and concepts that you think of as "clearly defined," and therefore you wouldn't normally bring up with customers. But never assume that any of your definitions are the same as the customer's (unless there are common industry standards you're using).

I once asked a room full of salespeople from one company what their strongest sales point was. They all replied "our quality data." I then asked them to each write down a definition of what "quality data" meant, and, you guessed it, they each had a different definition. If no two salespeople in the same company could agree, what are the odds that the customer would be interpreting "quality data" the same way that the salesperson does?

asking them "What are you trying to accomplish with this requirement?" One of my clients, for example, is an international laboratory service company. They often encounter prospective customers who say they want to work with a "small company" (or will say that my client's company is "too large"). Knowing that they may run into this issue, my client's salespeople have to be ready to probe customers on what it is they are trying to accomplish by working with a smaller company or to inquire why they object to dealing with bigger companies. With careful guidance, the customer will often talk about what lies behind the criterion of "working with a small company." What they want are often things like "personalized service" or "fast turnaround time" or "a single point of contact we can meet with locally." While my client can never become the "small company" that such customers initially say they require, they can meet these more specific criteria that underlie that request.

Trapping Competitors Inside "Intangibles"

Service, quality, and value are bantered around in every industry, but what do they really mean? Advertising today screams, "We have the best service," and "We have the best quality!" But how can they say this if their customer works the night shift and they're not open at 3 A.M.?

You can use this vagueness to your advantage if you're the first to help your customers to start thinking in more concrete terms.

For example, say your company touts its ability to provide "great service." You can't know if you do that unless you ask your clients, "What does great service mean to you?"

Usually what happens is that the customer realizes that their criteria around "great service" are intangible. This uncertainty can be used to your advantage in two ways. First, if you're the one that helps the customer think through and verbalize how they would recognize great service if they saw it, you can make sure that your company meets those criteria as much as possible.

Second, the next time your competitor comes in and brags about *their* service, the customer will then think, "How can this person say this? They don't know what great service means to me because they've never asked." At this point, your trap has been sprung on your competitor.

Creating a Better Match Between Criteria and Capabilities

In many cases you'll run into situations where at first blush the strengths of your offering are not considered significant by the customer and/or there are criteria the customer considers important that you know you can't meet.

If there is an easily measured, tangible criterion that you can't meet, there's not much you can do. A logistics company can't disguise the fact that they don't offer online tracking of shipments if that's something the customer considers important. A shared web services provider can't promise to support Mac operating systems if all it can handle is Windows. You can't tell customers you can offer twenty-four-hour resolution of problems if the data shows you need forty-eight hours or more.

But don't throw in the towel the first time you hear the customer mention something that isn't one of your strong points or that you're not sure your solution can provide. An expert architect has two strategies to draw on:

1. Getting customers to reevaluate their buying criteria (and perhaps shift the ranking of importance)
2. Finding alternative ways to satisfy a requirement

Option #1: Getting Customers to Reevaluate Their Buying Criteria

You have two tactics you can use to shift how customers rank their buying criteria: move something up the list, or move it down.

> **Escalate the importance of criteria in which you are superior.** Once you have identified your prospects' must-haves and nice-to-haves, you should emphasize the importance of criteria in which your product or service is superior (which you know from your market assessment). You want to help your prospects recognize the value of these criteria, especially if they represent an advantage for you over the competition.

> **Diminish the importance of nice-to-haves in which you are weak.** Don't put emphasis on nice-to-haves where you may be weak. Depending on your buyers' preference, the pendulum could swing either in your favor or against you. At this stage of the buying process, it's best to emphasize the importance of capabilities where you have a distinct advantage. The next chapter takes a closer look at how to deal with weaknesses that your buyers consider important.

Option #2: Finding Alternative Ways to Satisfy a Requirement

As I discussed in Step 4 of the Architect's Toolkit, the issues of how well your solution meets or doesn't meet a customer need often revolves around intangible and/or vague criteria.

You should already know in big-picture terms what the customer is trying to accomplish. Here, the focus is much narrower: what they are trying to accomplish with a particular criterion.

That's where your probing of *why* the customer includes each criterion comes in handy, because there may be other ways to achieve it. So I repeat the advice: Probe for details around *what* they want to be able to do and *how* they want to be able to do it. Also, ask about prior experiences that have led them to come up with their requirements. (For the lab services company mentioned earlier, the desire to work with a "small company" is likely linked to problems the company has had working with large companies in the past.)

If you encounter a criterion in which you are weak *and you know the reasons behind that criterion*, your first thought should be whether any of your strengths or differentiators can help support the reason behind that criterion. Failing that, you can put on your brainstorming hat and see if there are other things your company *can* do to meet the underlying need.

Say that the jet plane provider encounters a customer who rates "cabin comfort" very high in importance—but that was a characteristic where the provider ranked below average. Probing about why cabin comfort is important to the customer, they could hear a range of responses: "We have long overseas flights and want comfortable seats and couches" or "We ship teams of people around the country and we need a space where five people can meet around a table." If they get the former answer, they can leverage their faster speed (which equals shorter flights) as a factor that influences comfort on an overseas flight.

If they get the latter answer, they can explore cabin configurations and other features that would facilitate effective meetings during flights. One caveat: This kind of brainstorming should always be done offline, *not* in front of the customer. Once you've done your best to meet the needs, you can then go back to the customer to explore the options, or include the option you consider best in your proposal. Creativity is the Architect's tool for solving difficult design problems.

Create a Unique Solution to Match Customer Needs

If you don't know your customer's buying criteria, or if you find yourself guessing, consider it a signal that you haven't placed enough emphasis on uncovering customer needs. You will have added significant value to your customer's buying process if *they* come away with a better understanding of their buying criteria and with a greater awareness of important issues they had not previously considered.

If you want to achieve greater sales success, you have to participate in the creation of a unique solution that meets your customer's needs. When the solution you design for your prospect includes certain buying criteria that you are uniquely qualified to address, you have set the ground rules in your favor. But, in order to achieve this result, you must, again, resist the temptation to pitch your solution too soon. Instead, design a customer-focused solution that locks out your competition.

CHAPTER 7

The Coach

Make a Plan to Defeat the Competition

Recently, I was in the field with a salesperson who worked for the national accounts group of a large payroll processing firm. We were about to keep an appointment he'd made with the VP of human resources for a hospital with 3,000 employees. The salesperson told me the VP had called him the previous week, saying that she was interested in a new solution for employee benefits administration.

The salesperson expected a challenging situation because his company's strength was that they offered a single integrated solution that met human resource, employee benefits, and payroll processing needs. His company had different competitors within each component of that integrated solution. In other words, because he would be trying to sell the kitchen sink, he was anticipating a real problem, pricewise, selling to a customer who thought they only needed a new faucet.

Early in the meeting, the prospect reiterated her interest in finding a new solution for employee benefits administration. The salesperson responded by asking questions about her needs in the other areas of his integrated solution: HR, payroll processing, tax and compliance, etc. His questions were ineffective at developing the prospect's interest in other topics, and she remained fixated on her mental picture of an employee benefits solution. So, finally, the salesperson presented capabilities on his employee benefits product and agreed to follow up with a proposal.

As the meeting came to an end, the VP of HR said, "By the way, my director of training recently resigned, and I'm looking for a replacement. If you think of someone who might be a good fit please let me know." The salesperson said, "Sure. What are you looking for?" The VP responded with a comprehensive list of her requirements: minimum of ten years in organizational development, three years as a director of training in the healthcare field, experienced at hiring and managing in-house curriculum developers, proven ability to diagnose productivity problems, etc., etc.

Afterwards, the sales rep asked me, "How do you think that meeting went?" I replied, "Well, you now know more about her *hiring* criteria than her *buying* criteria." I told him that, in my opinion, he had sold too fast. He had been so focused on trying to push additional differentiators that he failed to find the customer needs those differentiators could address. His sales strategy was flawed and he had therefore ceded the sale to the person who had defined the playing field (the customer's requirement for an employee-benefit-only solution).

That kind of failure in selling skills is why I've advised repeatedly in recent chapters that when a customer tells you they have a need, slow down and probe for details about that need. Only by understanding the needs and the reasons underlying the solution requirements can you develop a winning strategy. Had this salesperson asked about the symptoms and causes underlying the HR VP's desire to change employee benefits administration, he may have discovered justification for at least some portion of an integrated solution. He didn't need to sell the entire kitchen sink to defeat the salesperson selling the faucet; the faucet plus just one more component would have been enough to knock any single-component competitors out of the game.

Unfortunately, many salespeople lack the knowledge and skills for defeating the competition; they are unable to convince customers their solution is best. They need the skills of a Coach who can analyze the competition, select an appropriate strategy, and create a game plan to win. This chapter is all about developing those skills for yourself so you can win more sales.

Evaluating Your Starting Position

A hallmark of professional selling is the assumption that you will face a lot of competition. Even if you have done business with a prospect in the past and have a good relationship with a former Sponsor, *do not assume* that will guarantee you a sale the next time around. Always assume that the prospect will shop around.

Luckily, if you initiated contact with a customer and guided them through the first three steps of their buying process (*Change, Discontent, Research*), then you are likely in a very strong position as they enter the fourth step, *Comparison*. Your in-depth knowledge of *all* their needs and your collaboration in shaping their mental picture of an ideal solution gives you a major edge over your competitors. **In fact, in your role of Architect, you have defined the playing field that you'll now compete on as a Coach.**

However, when a prospect contacts you—as was the case with the HR director mentioned above—it's critical to determine whether you're the first call they're making or the second (or third or fourth . . .). Frankly, the later you get involved in your customer's buying process, the lower your chances of winning because there is a distinct possibility that your customer has defined his or her needs based on an interaction with one of your competitors.

The obvious danger is that the competitor defined the needs in ways that favor their solution (you'd do the same, right?). But there is another danger. Paul Nutt, author of *Why Decisions Fail*, studied 400 executive decisions and found that nearly half failed—meaning either they were never implemented at all or had fallen by the wayside within a few years. A major contributor to this failure was the tendency for the executives to "latch onto" the first solution that was presented to them, closing their minds to other opportunities.[11]

Three Entry Points and Your Options

There are three possible scenarios you need to think about:

1. The customer is aware of the need to change (Buying Step 2, *Discontent*) and is beginning their *Research* (Step 3) to identify possible solutions. You are their first call, and they have no specific solution in mind. They want to learn from you.

2. The customer has already identified a specific solution on their own (they have completed Step 3 and are transitioning into Step 4, *Comparison*). You are the first call, but they already have a fairly specific solution in mind.

3. The customer worked with a competitor while doing their *Research*, and is now firmly in the *Comparison* step, where they are seeking information from multiple vendors. You are not their first call and they have a mental picture of a solution that was shaped by one of your competitors.

Scenario 1 is good news for you. It means you get to participate in helping the customer define the ideal solution. That means practicing the Doctor role (doing diagnostic questioning) and the Architect role (shaping their mental picture), as described in previous chapters.

Scenarios 2 and 3 are much more challenging. It is in *your* best interest to get the customer to repeat earlier steps in their buying process so that you get a clear understanding of their needs and can best evaluate where you stand relative to what the customer has in mind and what other competitors have presented as solutions. But the customer may be reluctant to take the time to repeat those steps.

Be Realistic About Your Odds

Another common mistake salespeople make when they're not the first in the door is that they overestimate their chances of winning the sale. They answer the customer's questions, present their product, and report to their boss that the sales opportunity has a 70 percent probability of success—when the actual odds may be less than 10 percent.

In fact, Keith Eades, author of *The New Solution Selling*, reports that the IBM Software Group found that it *lost sales 93 percent of the time when they were not involved in defining the requirements for the solution.*[12] So even for IBM's sophisticated sales staff, their odds of winning were as little as 7 percent. (This is another plug for prospecting. The more opportunities that *you* create, the higher your success percentage.) If you're lucky, however, your competitors will not have read this book, and they'll still be selling too fast and making the kinds of mistakes that will increase *your* odds of getting in the door and winning the sale.

I was recently contacted by a customer who was reaching out to multiple suppliers (the company was in the *Comparison* step). I never really had a chance of winning the sale in part because I couldn't get time with a key figure on a Complex Buying Team who was both the Power Broker and Gatekeeper (trying to protect the other eight people on the team from being bothered by us suppliers). That meant I had no opportunity to fully understand this client's needs or demonstrate how and why my company's offering could be an ideal solution.

What I should have done was said to this Power Broker/ Gatekeeper when I was first contacted, "I'm delighted about your interest in my company and the opportunity to submit a proposal. I need one hour of your time so I can be sure I fully understand your needs and determine whether or not we'd be a good match." I suspect she would have said no, which would have been a clear indicator that reaching out to me was simply a pro forma step done to satisfy her company's desire to have multiple bids. She had already made her choice.

If someone on a Complex Buying Team won't consider a reasonable request for a meeting, they are not seriously considering you as a supplier. Other warning signals that the decision makers may have already made a choice include:

- Use of terminology and performance criteria language that a competitor uses.

- Your key contact and other members of the Complex Buying Team are operating on a self-imposed short deadline (they cannot give you a compelling reason why the decision has to be made quickly; they just want to get it over with).

- You have a hard time making it past a Gatekeeper, and that person doesn't read the information you send them or respond to phone calls. If you do talk to the Gatekeeper, ask specific questions about their understanding of your solution. And pay attention to the Gatekeeper's tone of voice. It's a feeling you get that the Gatekeeper wants this meeting, or phone call, to be over.

- The company, even your Sponsor, is slow to respond to your requests for information.

- You don't even have a Sponsor, someone who wants you to succeed.

If you see any of these warning signals, you can still pursue the sale, but be realistic about your odds—realism will help you choose a better strategy.

Tip: Do Not Challenge a Preexisting Choice Directly

If you suspect the decision makers you're dealing with have been presented with, and latched onto, a solution, do not challenge that decision directly. That will just give them a reason to defend the choice they've already made. You can either abandon the sale, or take it as a challenge to develop a winning game plan despite having the odds running against you.

The takeaway from these examples is that you want to **be the first to define your customer's need and the solution,** if you can—which will happen only if you get better at prospecting. If you can't be first, you'll have to work harder. "Get into your customer's head" to help your customer see new opportunities in redefining the need.

In this chapter, I'll talk about what to do no matter whether you are encountering scenarios 2 or 3 (a customer that has potentially already made a choice) or have shepherded a customer through their earlier buying steps. I'll show you how to become a strong Coach skilled at developing a winning game plan. If you want to stop losing sales to competition then you've got to sharpen your **competitive** selling skills.

Customer Step 4: *Comparison*

Customers want to ensure that they make the best buying decision. Once they they have completed the *Research* step, they shop around.

When your customer is in the *Comparison* step, the step with the most competitive activity, you'll hear things like "What's different about your offering?" or "Why should I choose you?"

Understanding what happens with customers in the *Comparison* step will help you understand when and how you need to interact with them.

Many, if not most, Complex Buying Teams you'll encounter are going to be operating under a requirement that they generate two or more options before making a final decision. Sometimes that's because their company has a policy against sole-source acquisitions; other times it may just be a corporate standard to compare alternatives.

Either way, this means that in most cases a customer's Step 4, *Comparison*, goes through four phases:

1. Considering only options with must-have capabilities.
2. Requesting presentations.

3. Identifying additional nice-to-haves in each option.
4. Identifying a preference.

Phase #1: Consider Only Options with Must-Have Capabilities

Early in the *Comparison* step, your prospect's Gatekeeper (who almost certainly will have been appointed by now) will undoubtedly contact various suppliers. Options that do not meet the must-have capabilities are quickly eliminated, thereby simplifying (at least somewhat) a complex decision.

Because one must-have criterion is usually price, all options being considered usually fall within an acceptable "price range." For this reason, price often disappears (temporarily) as an issue during this step. (Remember, the ROI Authority is now in the background, delegating the evaluation of options to people closer to the problem.) Instead, the buyer's focus is on identifying differences between alternatives in areas other than price. If the buyer fails to recognize a significant difference between acceptable alternatives (differences considered important by the Buying Team), their buying decision will be based on the most obvious difference: lowest price.

Phase #2: Request Presentations

Next, your prospect will evaluate different options by requesting presentations, or at least a clear description of your solution. The buyer's primary question is: "What is our best choice?"

Phase #3: Identify Additional Nice-to-Haves in Each Solution

As potential solutions are examined, the customer continues learning and will identify additional differences between alternative solutions that they consider important. This is one way in which buying criteria evolve, and you should keep on top of the changing situation.

Tip: Don't Respond Blindly to RFPs

If you sell to businesses, somewhere during the *Comparison* step your prospects may send out a Request for Proposal (RFP) or ask you to make a formal sales presentation. Here's an important tip: if the RFP is the first you've heard about the opportunity, it means you're entering the game late (whether or not there are other competitors) and the odds of winning are low.

David Ullman tells a story in *Making Robust Decisions* about a company that sent out an RFP to multiple suppliers. The suppliers all jumped through many hoops and bent over backwards to submit detailed, voluminous proposals. Once the company read through all the proposals, they realized they'd botched the original RFP, and it was back to the drawing board.

The way I handle the situation is to call up the customer and say, "Thank you for sending the RFP. I need an hour of your time to ask some questions and fully understand if we would be a good fit for your needs." If the customer says no, I know there is little chance I can make a sale. If they are unwilling to give me one hour of their time, why should I spend twenty hours responding to an RFP?

Phase #4: Identify a Preference

Step 4, *Comparison*, concludes when the buyer identifies their preferred option—hopefully yours.

When customers are in Step 4, you'll need to put into play everything you've learned about their needs, plus your knowledge of your own product or service and what the competition is offering.

Eventually, you'll have to capture what you know about the customer and the solution you envision in a proposal or presentation. I'll discuss that milestone in the next chapter; before you get to the point of putting anything down in writing, you need to develop a strategy for winning the game.

How a Coach Develops a Winning Game Plan

The buying-focused selling role that matches the prospect's Step 4, *Comparison*, is the **Coach**. A salesperson's objective in the Coach sales role is to win with honesty and integrity.

If you've been schooled in a traditional, sales-process–focused sales approach, be fore-warned that even now you'll have to fight the temptation to sell too fast. You now clearly see the customer's need and sorely want to talk about your product or service. But if you jump the gun by providing prospects with all the in-formation about your product or service immediately there will be no compelling reason for them to continue discussions with you. This means that for all practical purposes, you finish selling and therefore disconnect from your customers at the very moment when competitors arrive on the scene. By carefully pacing the amount of in-formation you deliver and instead continuing to ask more questions from the Architect's Toolkit as you develop your winning strategy, you'll stay in touch with your customers at this critical stage of the customer's learning.

The best Coaches first evaluate the players involved: your cus-tomer, your competitors, and, of course, your own team. Then a Coach selects a competitive strategy, a game plan, to defeat the com-petition. Once the game begins, the Coach must stay flexible, mak-ing adjustments to the game plan as more information becomes available about what the competition is doing and what the cus-tomer is thinking.

Scouting the Competition

One major difference between a winning sales game plan and a win-ning football game plan is that in football, it's easy to identify your competition. That's not the case in selling. Your competitors don't wear different-colored jerseys—and they don't hunker down across from you.

How can you identify the competition you are up against? The simplest way is to ask your Sponsor.

Another tactic is to pay close attention to your prospects' objections. Objections are often echoes of things a competitor has said about you, your products/services, and/or your company. Street-smart salespeople are sensitive to these objections. They not only indicate who you are up against, but what their sales strategies are.

Still another method for identifying competitors is to ask your prospect, "What steps have you taken thus far in regards to making this decision?" If the prospect answers that they've already begun evaluating options from various suppliers, say, "May I ask, what capabilities have you seen from other suppliers that would be important components of your solution?" They may say they're not comfortable sharing that information, but in many cases they will talk about specific capabilities suggested by a competitor, which should provide you with a clue as to who that competitor is.

If you are continually going up against the same competitors, you probably have already done your scouting homework and figured out how they are going to sell against you. If not, here are five steps to help you get started:

> Look at your competitors' advertisements, websites, and sales brochures. Make a detailed list of each opponent's selling points.

> Ask your existing customers, who previously evaluated your solution, what factors affected their decision. Talk to them and ask why you were selected.

> Interview coworkers who are recent defectors from competing companies as soon as they have joined your company, while their memories are fresh.

> List the most common objections you hear about your solution—and determine which can be traced back to your competitors.

▷ Create a list of the advantages you believe your competitors consider their strengths. This will help you figure out how they're going to sell against you.

Tip: Look at Your Toughest Competitors

One football coach I interviewed said that before each season started he looked at his ten-game schedule and picked the three toughest competitors. He then installed a system for the entire season that stood the best chance of beating his three toughest opponents. You should consider doing the same.

Now that you know who you're up against—and what their sales strategy is likely to be—it's time to determine exactly how your solution compares to theirs.

Doing a Competitive Analysis

As an Architect of selling during buyers' Step 3, *Research*, you identified typical buying criteria by conducting a market assessment (see Table 6-2, page 117) and evaluating your strengths and weaknesses against the marketplace in *general* (because Step 3 usually occurs *before* competition is involved). You then influenced your prospects' criteria to include your unique strengths. If you did a good job, these criteria are the standards against which suppliers will be measured now that the customer is in Step 4, *Comparison*.

As a Coach, you need to find out what your direct opponents are offering and use these same criteria to identify their strengths and weaknesses. I call this activity a **competitive analysis**. An example, building on the eight-passenger corporate jet started in the previous chapter, is shown in Table 7-1.

If competing alternatives are judged by a buyer as being equal with regard to a certain capability, then the decision maker will shift focus to the remaining differences between alternatives that are considered important. For example, if all three corporate jet

Table 7-1 Competitive Assessment on an Eight-Passenger Corporate Jet

BUYING CRITERIA THE CUSTOMER IDENTIFIED (PRIORITIZED)	COMPETITORS / RATINGS			ADVANTAGE
	BRAND A	BRAND B	BRAND C	
Range (in miles)	3070 A	3250 S	3000 A	Brand B
Cruising speed	Mach .92 SS	Mach .8 A	Mach .8 A	Brand A
Take-off distance (in feet)	5140 S	5878 SBA	5000 S	Brand C
Cabin comfort	Few options BA	Some options A	Most options S	Brand C
Price (in million $)	$10 S	$10.75 A	$11.5 SBA	Brand A
Support capabilities	24/7/365 A	24/7/365 A	24/7/365 A	——
Brand recognition	A	BA	S	Brand C

A = average
S/SS = superior/significantly superior
BA = below average
SBA = significantly below average

suppliers are judged as having acceptable 3,000-mile range, then range goes away as a buying criterion. It is still important to the buyer, but it doesn't help them choose between potential suppliers. Instead, the buyer shifts focus to other differences deemed important.

Don't limit your competitive analysis to a list of features. Simply comparing your product or service against a competitor's offering is like comparing a quarterback to a cornerback: it doesn't take into account *all* the positions on the field.

To see how this approach works, think of one of your prospects

Tip: Include Criteria from All Decision Makers

When doing your competitive analysis, be sure to include criteria that reflect the requirements of all decision makers on the Complex Buying Team—operational requirements of interest to users, compatibility information of interest to the Integrator, purchase price and full lifecycle costs for the ROI Authority, and so on.

who's shopping around and ask yourself the following questions (you're going to need this information when you develop a sales proposal/presentation):

> What's my understanding of their buying criteria?
> What's most important to my prospect? What's next most important? And next?
> Which of those criteria represent a competitive edge for me?
> Which criteria represent a competitive disadvantage for me?
> Who's positioned most favorably at this time—me or my competition?
> What can I do to influence the customer's criteria so that they'll see a better match between my offering and their needs?
> What are three reasons why this customer should buy from me instead of my competition?

If you don't know the answers to these questions, then figure out how you can get back in there and find out.

Tip: Ask Recent Purchasers for Help

People who recently bought from you after scouting the competition are a rich source of information. It's worth talking to them to see what they can tell you about how your product or service compares to the rest of the market. Ask them if they would explain why they chose you, what strengths *they* perceived. If you know them well, ask if they will send you copies of your competitors' proposals.

Five Winning Strategies

If you've been with your customer through their earlier stages of buying, you will have had a hand in helping shape their buying criteria, so it's the competition who should be worried, not you. If you are just entering the game in the *Comparison* step, your game plan is going to have to involve working with the customer to redefine the requirements in your favor.

There are five basic strategies for winning a new account. Choosing the right strategy for the dynamics of the specific situation gives you the best chance of winning. Here is a quick overview; I'll get to more details right afterwards:

1. **Drive straight up the middle.** If your team is stronger than the competition, then you want to take a direct approach. Overpower the competition by emphasizing your strengths and minimizing your weaknesses. The sooner in a buying process you become involved, the better your chances of winning with this strategy. If you were involved from the beginning, meaning if you created this opportunity, you have already been implementing the "up the middle strategy." (The Architect role is essentially part of such a strategy because you help to design the customer's mental picture of a solution.)

2. **Run a reverse.** Coaches call this the "misdirection" play. If your competitor has the customer leaning in a certain direction, you fake in the same direction, then suddenly reverse to go in a different direction. Run around the opposition in a flanking maneuver by redesigning the customer's mental picture of what they're trying to accomplish.

    In describing the difference between management and leadership, author Steven Covey says, "Management is efficiency in climbing the ladder of success; leadership determines whether the ladder is leaning against the right wall."[13] If your competitor was first in the door, they have been managing the ladder of the customer's buying process. But is your customer's ladder leaning up against the right wall? Would your customer be better served by pursuing a new and different mental picture? (Note: This strategy works best if you have a strong Sponsor in the account.)

3. **Throw your challenge flag.** In professional football, if a coach thinks the referees made a mistake in calling the play—that how referees saw the play is, in the coach's opinion, incorrect—he can throw a red challenge flag. The goal with the challenge flag is to delay the game to give the referees a chance to check instant replay video and determine if they made a mistake. When you, as the competitive sales coach, employ this strategy your goal is the same: to delay the decision. If you can delay just a few months, the customer's players (decision makers), their business needs, or even the economy may be different, opening up new avenues.

4. **Take what the defense gives you.** If you decide that you can't win the opportunity as it is currently defined, go after a small piece of it. (This is also sometimes called the "beachhead" approach.) See if you can convince your customer that a "hybrid" solution might serve them best—combining a component of the solution that you do really well with other components from the leading competitor. In this way you gain access to the account and, over time, will have the opportunity to build the relationships that you need to be considered for larger, more sophisticated projects.

5. **Take advantage of sticker shock.** Sometimes (and more often than you might think), your competitors will fail to establish budget limits up front. Then, when they submit their proposal, the prospect goes into sticker shock. If you are prepared, you can slip in the door while the customer is reevaluating. If you're not the *first* salesperson in the door, make sure you know if a budget has been determined for the investment.

In general, you'll want to use an up-the-middle strategy if your competitive analysis has shown that you're in a strong position. If you're in a weak position, consider one of the others. Let's take a closer look at each.

Tip: Stay Close to Your Sponsors

Nowhere in the buying process is having a close relationship with a Sponsor more important than when your prospect is in the *Comparison* step. You need to have someone who will answer the "Where do I stand?" question honestly, and help you understand how your proposed solution may fall short compared to the competition . . . and then give you advice on how to win up the middle, play a reverse, or settle for whatever piece of the action you can get.

Strategy #1: Drive Straight Up the Middle

You're first in the door and have framed the customer's mental picture of a solution. Now, as your competitors arrive on the scene, you must continue to strengthen your team's position by continuing to paint the customer's mental picture of a solution in more clear and vivid terms. Many of the same strategies and tactics you used during the Architect role will work here as a Coach.

At this point in the selling process, your prospect is considering many buying criteria, some of which are strengths for you, others of which may be weaknesses. Because your overall competitive position is determined by the sum total of your various strengths and weaknesses, a winning game plan consists of several strategies, not just one. **You may need to call a different play for each customer criterion.** Which play you call depends on your relative position. If the circumstances of one criterion are different from those of another, two different plays are needed. Here I'll describe five play options you can include in an "up the middle" game plan, using the jet plane example set up in Table 7-1.

1. **Repackage weaknesses by adding favorable criteria to the buyer's list**. Suppose you're the Brand C salesperson. Your price is higher than your two main competitors. Big problem.

But you have resale numbers that show that after seven years of operation, your jet will be worth $1 million more in resale value. So, really, the price difference is "just" $500K against your strongest price competitor. Shouldn't the resale value be considered along with purchase price?

2. **Emphasize and enhance your strengths**. If you're selling for Brand C you have a big advantage over Brand A in terms of cabin comfort. Ask more questions around this issue. Define "cabin comfort" in more tangible terms consistent with your strengths.

3. **Link your solution to the customer's existing equipment/processes.** Does the prospect already own other models in your brand line? That could mean less training for pilots, and less need to purchase different parts or tools for repairs they could handle themselves. Do you have repair facilities located in more airports that your prospect will be using?

4. **Correct your customer's misconceptions**. Always be on the lookout for customer misunderstandings, which may have been created by your competitors' mistruths and half-truths.

5. **Look for weaknesses in your competitor's strengths**. If you're selling for Brand C, yes, Brand B has a higher cruising speed. But that means lower fuel economy and, for the eco-sensitive buyer, a larger carbon footprint.

If you're selling to the Complex Buying Team, the order in which each decision maker ranks the criteria may well be different. You put yourself in a stronger competitive position by considering each decision maker's priorities separately, identifying at least three reasons why you're the best choice for each of these different decision makers, then using the above plays to decide on the best combination for each decision maker.

Look again at Table 7-1 and put yourself in the position of selling Brand A jets. Your most significant weakness is likely "cabin

---

Tip: Revert to Being an Architect When Needed

The Architect chapter mentioned that the criteria customers will use to make the final buying decision (which solution to choose from which vendor) can shift over time. I hope you are keeping in touch with your Sponsor(s) and can check in with them regularly to see if they have added criteria, made some criteria more or less important than originally thought, eliminated some criteria, etc.

Even when acting in your Coach role, draw on the Architect's toolkit (pages 118–124) to flesh out the criteria:

- Diagnostic probing (if needed).
- Establishing the solution criteria.
- Planting a seed.
- Turning intangibles into tangibles; turning vague criteria into specifics.

---

comfort" (unless the extra 140 feet of takeoff distance compared to Brand C affects the airports that can be accessed). You will need to determine how to talk about cabin comfort because it will likely come up in conversations with prospects. Otherwise, three ways you could win with an up-the-middle strategy are:

- You know that you have an edge in avionics, although that was not a criterion identified by the customer. (Your plane's avionics system has a unique feature for stability during strong turbulence.) You could introduce additional criteria by planting the seed in the customer's mind about the potential need for "bad weather capabilities." (This might be important to any Users of the jets, including likely pilots.)
- Redefine "support capabilities" to mean that you will provide the customer with the name and phone number for experts responsible for each aspect of the plane's operation (avionics, brakes, engine, etc.).
- Raise the issue of your jet engines, which are manufactured by one of the world's best-known and leading brands.

Tip: Consider Role Playing These Strategies

A number of sales professionals have told me that they are more comfortable using these up-the-middle game plays in real situations if they'd tried them out first by role playing with some colleagues. We do that as a standard part of our seminars, and people find it useful to have to put into concrete language something they had previously only envisioned in theory.

Strategy #2: Run a Reverse

A colleague recently asked me how often I used the reverse play. My gut instinct was to say "rarely," but when I thought more about it, I realized that I use a Reverse strategy almost every time *I'm not the first in the door.* The discussion earlier in this chapter should give you the clue why: by coming into the process late, I have to assume that my competitors have set the requirements for the customer's solution. The only way I can win is to open the door just a crack so the customer begins to entertain the possibility of alternatives. Then I adopt both the Doctor role (using effective diagnostic questions) and the Architect role (to construct a new mental picture for the buyer).

One secret to being successful with Reverse plays is to think of ways your customer could achieve greater results than even they are envisioning. Consider existing customers who have implemented your solution in new and different ways, the customers who gained much greater value from your product or service than others. What are these "uber-customers" doing differently from other customers? If the answer to that question is a different concept than what the current prospect is considering, it's your professional responsibility to introduce the game-changing concept to them. Also, make a list of the most unique solutions you've delivered for customers. What specific differences does your company have, or could you have, and how can you make these differences important to your buyer?

As soon as you sense that your competitor did a good job of painting the customer's mental picture, *that* is the time to call the reverse play. Don't put it off, because the longer you wait the lower your chances of success.

There are two motivations for calling the Reverse. First, you want to win. Second, you are motivated by a desire to help your customers achieve greater value by going in a different direction—by defining a different need. That's why you need to act fast; the further away you get from the customer's Need stage, the lower your chances of success with the Reverse. It looks to the customer like an act of desperation.

Suppose, for example, that you're selling Brand C jets, which have a higher price. If a customer perceives the options as equal except for your higher price (because they don't value your other strengths), you need to develop a new scenario. You know you have an alternative to offer your customers: the potential to purchase a *share* in multiple jets from your company, then pay a monthly fee and hourly operation costs. On as little as four hours' notice, your company can then send out whichever size jet your customer needs that is most conveniently located. Need a twelve-seat jet next week in Paris? No problem. Need three jets the week after that in Rio? No problem.

Now the competitive situation is completely reversed. Why should the customer spend $10+ million on any *one* jet, plus costs for insurance, fuel, pilots, and catering, when they could have access to a fleet of jets for a fraction of the up-front costs?

Be forewarned, though. Reverse plays can be risky. If done wrong, the customer will think that you're *ignoring* their needs rather than trying to redefine them!

Strategy #3: Throw a Challenge Flag

Another option you can use if you sense a competitor is likely to win is to persuade your customer to delay their decision. Usually the "hook" you need to delay the decision is to plant seeds of doubt about the future. For customers, a common mistake made during a buying process is focusing in the present. Customers have evaluated solutions to determine which solution is the best option *today*, but often haven't considered the *future* and how their needs may be different six to twelve months from now.

To throw a challenge flag, ask your customer to look out a year and think about changes already under way in their business or potential changes that may be coming inside or outside their company. For example, will they be upgrading technology? Going through other major organizational changes? Will a supplier be upgrading or changing their deliverable in a way that could add greater value if the customer waits before making this purchase? Suppose you sell wireless services, and your company's wireless network will be upgraded starting later this year, bringing numerous new capabilities and applications to your customer. You connect your "future" to the customer's needs, encouraging the customer to delay.

An added benefit of this strategy is its likely effect on your competitor's salesperson who confidently thinks he or she has all but won the sale. When the customer buying wheel suddenly grinds to a halt, the salesperson in the number-one position pushes harder to try and close the sale. This can cause that competitor to lose credibility with the customer, leaving you in a much stronger position a few months down the road.

Strategy #4: Take What the Defense Gives You

All of us have been in situations where it's clear that we're not going to be the top choice for the main solution that has been envisioned. Yes, our odds of winning the whole sale are low, but that doesn't mean we should give up.

Remember the story at the opening of the chapter of a salesperson's unsuccessful attempt to "reverse" the VP of HR's mental picture of an employee benefit solution? Suppose, for a moment, that the salesperson had been successful at the Reverse—changing the vision of an ideal solution to include the full kitchen sink (it will address human resource, employee benefits, and payroll processing needs).

Now put yourself in the place of one salesperson who is selling just a faucet, only part of this new solution. You sense that you cannot win based on the new customer buying criteria, so you just go after the employee benefits piece of business. Assuming your employee benefits package is superior and can be seamlessly integrated with the competitor's payroll and HR components, your goal is to win the portion of the customer's business that you can do best.

Once you are in the door, you can build important relationships, measure your success, and communicate that success to key decision makers—what I refer to as the Farmer role (Chapter 11). As you know, it's a lot easier to sell an existing customer than a new one. Best of all, the customer wins because she achieves her goal of an integrated solution consisting of the best possible individual components.

Another option if you find yourself in a potential losing situation is to ask your Sponsor to pick one particular differentiator, one capability of your solution that they consider important, and plant their feet on that one issue. Dr. David Ullman wrote a book about how a Complex Buying Team can make better decisions. He writes in *Making Robust Decisions: Decision Management for Technical, Business, and Service Teams*: "Let's say that you can see that a decision is not going your way. You've already decided on your favorite alternative, but it doesn't look like it will be chosen. What can you do? You can micromanage the situation by finding a criterion that your favorite alternative satisfies very well and exaggerating its importance."[14] So essentially your Sponsor says to the rest of the Complex Buying Team, "You guys can pick what you want, but it has to have _____."

As you can probably tell, the only way this strategy—take what the defense gives you—works is if your solution or some part of your solution is compatible with whatever else your client is considering.

Tip: Pick a Game Plan Early

I've seen a lot of salespeople try a Reverse play or start maneuvering for a small piece of the overall solution. Most of the time they fail. Why? Because they wait until it's too late, until after the prospect has essentially made a decision not in their favor. The way to win with any of the strategies presented in this chapter is to **choose the appropriate strategy as early as possible—and certainly *before* you make a sales presentation or submit a proposal.**

How will you decide which path represents your best chance for winning? By talking to your Sponsors.

Strategy #5: Take Advantage of Sticker Shock

An executive I know told me recently that a new SVP of sales had joined his firm the previous summer and launched a process to hire a new sales training firm. The SVP's preference was for a company he had experience working with. He and the decision-making team evaluated that firm and one other company (neither of which was mine). They went through their *Research* and *Comparison* steps, requested in-person presentations, and then got the sales proposals. Their first choice wanted over $2 million! Ouch! They decided to delay the purchase since they didn't have $2 million in the budget. That delay will now give me time to get in the door.

What's ironic about the two companies that had been bidding is that the sales methods they teach includes an early step of defining if the budget had been approved for this investment. Not only had the budget not been approved in this case, but the customer had no clue how much the solution would cost. And yet both sales training companies proceeded with the sales process, flying teams thousands of miles to deliver big presentations. What a waste.

Become a Stronger Competitor

Coaches say that when two teams are evenly matched, the winner will be the team that executes its plays the best—the team that makes the fewest mistakes. That's why coaches spend a lot of time on a practice field, improving old skills and learning new ones. To win competitive sales, you must do the same. Coaches also know that, no matter how much time and energy they invest, they can't win them all. Everyone who competes has suffered defeat. So when you lose a sale, look for the lessons, adjust your activities accordingly, and move onward toward your goals.

What I'm saying is you've got to spend less time trying to close the sale—and more time positioning your solution as the customer's best choice. As I said before, if you don't know by this point in the sales process *at least three reasons* why your customer should buy from you—reasons that have been connected to explicit customer needs (so you know they're important to your customer)—then you have no right to ask for the business. If you have done your homework, however, now is the time to put your understanding to the acid test of preparing a convincing proposal or presentation, as I'll discuss in the upcoming Milestone.

MILESTONE #3

Winning Proposals and Presentations

Usually sales proposals and presentations enter the picture when the prospect is completing their *Comparison* step. The key question customers have at this stage of the buying decision is, who is our best choice? That is the question you're trying to answer by developing a proposal or presentation that describes a solution best matched to the customer's explicit needs.

Many salespeople have the mindset that they are "solution providers." But you can't tell it by their sales proposals or presentations. A *solution* is defined as "the answer to a problem"—so you'd think a "solution provider" is solving a problem, right? Take a look at most proposals and presentations, however, and what you'll see is a thorough description of predefined features/benefits of a product or service. The proposal/presentation usually communicates nothing about the prospect's problem that the "solution" is trying to solve!

What's the secret to writing proposals and presentations that will stand out from your competitors? **Provide clear descriptions**

153

of the prospect's problems, challenges, or opportunities you've seen (using the customer's language) and link your differentiating capabilities to the specific needs of that prospect. Do not simply provide generic statements of benefits.

By the time you reach the point of making a presentation or submitting a proposal, you should already have a good idea of:

- The members of your prospect's Complex Buying Team (as described in Chapter 2)

- The prospect's specific needs (discovered through diagnostic questioning and captured in the Memo of Understanding)

- Criteria important to each member of the team (developed through your Architect role)

- Where you stand against your competition and what your best game plan will be (the competitive analysis you completed in your Coach role)

If you are missing any of this information, you may be selling too fast. Slow down and fill in the gaps. If you do have this information, draw on it as you prepare your proposal or presentation to demonstrate that you understand the prospect's needs better than your competitors, and that you have the superior solution.

No matter whether the key milestone at this point is a presentation or proposal or both, the basic preparation is the same. The Proposal/Presentation Worksheet (next page) has a list of questions that can help you organize all the information you've gathered.

Developing a Convincing Proposal

When I engage with a new sales training client, my first request is for them to send me what they consider to be their three best sales proposals. A sales proposal captures the way a salesperson is describing their company's solution to the customer; seeing client examples

Proposal/Presentation Worksheet

1. What are the customer's three most serious problems, and why are they considered serious? What needs are they trying to meet?

2. What is my present understanding of this client's decision-making criteria? What is most important? What is the next most important? Which capabilities will we present that match this client's needs? *Hint: List them side-by-side (as shown below). Focus on the five or six capabilities most crucial to achieving this customer's goal. Don't overwhelm the client!*

Client's Criteria in Order of Importance	Matching Capabilities We Will Present

3. Which of these criteria represent a competitive edge for me? How will I emphasize these issues?

4. Which of these criteria represent a potential disadvantage for me? What is my plan for dealing with this?

5. What lingering intangible issues need to be defined in more tangible terms? *Hint: Decide how to resolve these issues. Confirm that you and the client are defining each need and solution criterion in the same way.*

6. Who is our # 1 competitor for this account? What are three reasons why this client should go with us instead of our competitor, and how will we connect these reasons to the client's explicit needs?

helps me gain a better understanding of how their salespeople sell. As I mentioned at the start of this chapter, nine out of ten proposals fail to link the capabilities of the seller's solution to explicit customer needs (needs the customer described, in *their* terms).

For example, one proposal I read recently stated that "Our focus will be on raising the bar within your Operations Department and empowering your personnel with robust data that can be used to reduce chargebacks." My questions about this big fat claim were:

1. What problems exist within this client's Operations Department that you can solve?
2. Specifically, why does this client currently experience chargebacks? What types of chargebacks would be reduced by your more robust data, and by how much?
3. Your answers to questions 1 and 2 need to be differentiated from competitors, both major national competitors as well as "regional low-balls." **Every capability you present that is not sufficiently differentiated from your competition moves you closer to a price war, but no closer to winning the sale.**

When was the last time your company took a hard look at your sales proposals? The value your company provides to customers likely changes over time. Has your sales proposal changed, too? Does your sales proposal persuasively communicate that you are the preferred solution provider in your marketplace?

Your proposal should reflect all of the information you have gathered on the prospect. For example, one of our clients sells workers' compensation insurance to corporations. These are annual policies that sell for between $200,000 and $2 million, depending on the number of employees and the likelihood of injuries on the job. The typical Buying Team they sell to includes the CFO (the ROI Authority, who makes the final decision), the director of HR (a Super User, responsible for handling claims), and Facilities Engineering (Integrator/technical expert, responsible for worker safety and loss control). The formal part of the sales proposal binder had five sections:

1. Your Financial Goals—and how we can achieve them.
2. Your Claims Services needs—and our solution.
3. Your Loss Control Needs—and our solution.
4. Why we're your best choice.
5. Suggested questions to ask each supplier.

The binder also included separate handouts of a sample implementation plan and a pricing page that were discussed separately.

The first four items above should be self-evident, but you may be wondering about the fifth item—questions for suppliers. As the label implies, this is a list of questions we are recommending the customer ask of all the suppliers they are comparing. It's a tactic I recommend to all salespeople as a mechanism for forcing your competitors to talk about issues they may not want to emphasize (issues related to your differentiators, for example). Common questions on such a list include:

> Can we select our own references to call from your customer list? *(This is a critical question. Every company, every salesperson has some clients that they know are successful and would love you to call. The question is whether they are comfortable enough to let the prospect select whom to call.)*

> How will you ensure a successful transition, with no business interruption?

> What do you do to measure the value of your services to your customers?

> What relevant experience do you have with clients similar to us?

Other questions will be specific to your industry and market.

A list like this is both customer-serving and self-serving: It is customer-serving in the sense that it can genuinely help your client make a more educated buying decision. (Remember, you are involved in this type of purchasing decision a lot more often than they are, and so you know more about what information will help them best predict the fit for both their short- and long-term needs.) It is self-serving in the sense that planting the right questions can be an effective part of your winning game plan (developed as a Coach) and help emphasize your differentiators that are most closely linked to the customer's needs.

I've used a proposal structure similar to this a number of times. Whether it is appropriate for you will depend on what types of decision makers will be reading your proposals. In general, pick a structure that reflects the interests of those decision makers, and when developing the detailed content, remember to think about where those decision makers typically are in their buying process at the moment you deliver or present your proposal.

You may have noted that I did not include an Executive Summary in the above proposal structure, and I don't recommend that you use them either. An Executive Summary provides an easy out that enables executives to learn very little about their needs and focus all their time on the pricing page. If you design your proposal to match the needs of different members of the Complex Buying Team, you are still allowing executives to jump directly to the section that addresses their primary issues and concerns. But hopefully they will pick up more key points about why your solution is structured the way it is and the total value it offers their company.

Tip: Other Uses of Your Preparation and Proposals

Once you have compiled the information needed to prepare a successful proposal, that work can help you in two other ways:

1. While you can't use it as an exact boilerplate (no two proposals will be identical because no two clients are identical), you should be able to pick up key points (such as explanations of your core strengths) to use in future proposals.

2. When you do this exercise—focusing on the problems, issues, and criteria by decision-maker type—what you then have is a template for diagnostic questioning during the Doctor role.

Presentations: Preparation Will Meet Opportunity

Generally there are two types of presentations: Some prospects will ask you to simply "deliver" the proposal you have developed. Others may want a full presentation (with flipcharts, PowerPoint slides, etc.) instead of, or in addition to, handing out a proposal.

If you plan to simply walk through your proposal, keep the pricing page and example implementation plan separate. Hand them out toward the end of your presentation. That will help you keep the discussion focused on needs/problems and solutions instead of price.

If you are asked to deliver a presentation, your preparation should start the same as any contact you have with a prospect: by determining the specific action you want the customer to take afterwards. Here, the answer will depend on where you come in the sequence of presenters:

- If you are first (or maybe second), the action you want is for them to ask the "suggested questions" of the competitors who follow you.
- If you're last, it is unlikely that the customer will commit to the purchase then and there, **but you *can* ask "Is there any reason why I shouldn't be your first choice?"** Assuming you do a good job of answering their questions and concerns, you'll know that the customer will exit this *Comparison* work with a positive impression of you and your company.

For example, in one of the largest sales opportunities I've ever worked on, my team was the third of three presenting to a committee of seven decision makers, the most senior of whom was the executive vice president. Just ten minutes before my conclusion, Mr. Burns (the executive VP) stood up, saying he had a plane to catch and his cab had arrived.

I said, "Mr. Burns, before you leave, may I ask you one final question?"

He said, "Sure."

"Can you think of any reason why our sales training solution would *not* be your best choice?" I asked.

He said, "Yep!"—and out it came—his final concern about our solution.

It was a concern that I was ready for, one I'd anticipated and could answer—but I never got the chance to respond to it. His comment triggered a firestorm of conversation around the conference table. As it turned out, Mr. Burns missed his cab, but several other decision makers drove him to the airport so they could continue their discussion. A few weeks later I learned that a lower-level decision maker had resolved his concern when they were in the car—and I won the sale! (This is another example justifying the claim that as much as 90 percent of the sale can take place when you're not there. So you've got to make sure that your Sponsors have the tools to sell other decision makers for you.)

These issues explain why **I advise going first or last.** Actually, let me be more specific. When I feel I've done an excellent job designing the customer's solution, then I prefer to go last because I *want* the prospect to be comparing the full picture of what my company is offering to what the competition has already brought out. But there are some situations where I haven't been able to fully design what I consider to be an optimal solution for the prospect, perhaps because my company wasn't contacted until late in the buying process or there were decision makers I was unable to talk with directly. In those cases, I want to be first so I can use some "suggested questions to ask the other suppliers" to plant the seed for alternative criteria or factors I think the client should be considering.

Once you know the outcome you want, identify the best way to get to that point through your presentation. The action you request of your prospect at the end of the meeting should be a logical next step. If the prospect fails to agree to this step, you have an early warning signal that all is not well.

Here are some additional tips on what to do as you develop your presentation.

1. **Find out in advance how much time you'll have.** You aren't holding the attention of a prospect who's looking at the clock! Have you ever had a key decision maker leave in the middle of your presentation because he or she was out of time? Plan your presentation to take more no more than 60 percent of the allotted time. Why so little? Because your prospect's decision to act typically happens at the end of a meeting, and you want to allow enough time to resolve any remaining issues and reach an agreement.

2. **Ask your Sponsor, "Since the last time we talked, has anything changed?"** If your competitor gave a presentation yesterday, you may have a few new hurdles to overcome. And the sooner you know what those hurdles are, the more time you have to plan your response.

3. **Ask your prospect, "Where are you in your decision process?"** This will help you determine what action to seek, as described above. If they tell you they've scheduled presentations with three suppliers, and you're the first presenter, you know the chance of them coming to a decision at the end of your presentation is virtually nil.

4. **Prepare an agenda (and use it).** Lay out the main topics of your presentation and how much time you think each will take (see the 60 percent rule above).

5. **Prepare a flip chart that lists the customer's goals/buying criteria.** List them in priority order.

6. **Get a sample implementation plan (one from a different client).** All clients have concerns about implementation (How long will it take? What's involved?). But realize that in order for them to embrace implementation, they have to be part of the planning. So you don't want to include a draft implementation plan for that specific client because they won't accept it (and it's likely you don't know enough to do a good job of drafting the plan anyway). Showing them a sample plan from another implementation will help them get a feel for what's involved without implying that it will work the exact same way for them.

7. **Rehearse.** Your presentation must be carefully planned and rehearsed. Never wing it!

Be Sure to Maintain Communication

Delivery of a sales proposal or presentation feels like an ending point of sorts for salespeople because it marks the culmination of a lot of work they have done. But it's often a starting point for increased activity among the Complex Buying Team. Now they have concrete proposals they must compare as they near the time to make a decision.

During this time when your customer is transitioning from exploration to decision, it is absolutely critical that you keep in touch with your Sponsor both immediately afterwards (to do a quick debrief on how you're doing relative to the competition) and continuing into the future, for two reasons.

First, **your Sponsor can use support and guidance as they become your champion inside their company.** Your Sponsor may need to sell your solution to other decision makers, particularly the ROI Authority. You may recall from Chapter 2 that the ROI Authority may be just reentering the process, having delegated the research and comparison work to the rest of the buying team.

If the ROI Authority actually attended your presentation, you have a leg up because he or she would have heard your best arguments directly from you. But in many cases, it may be your Sponsor(s) who will need to convince the ROI Authority that:

➢ Making this purchase is a priority. Remember, ROI Authorities often have a broad scope of responsibility and may be comparing investment in your solution against very different kinds of investments.

➢ Your option is the best solution.

For example, the VP of sales for a national firm gave the OK for a team operating under the chief learning officer (CLO) to investigate options for delivering training to the firm's sales force. This VP clearly told the team that he had a lot on his plate and sales training was no higher than second or third on his list of priorities.

Flash forward four months, and the team had done its research, gotten proposals from several suppliers (including our company), and was ready to make a recommendation to the VP of sales. No suppliers (including me) would be present at the recommendation meeting, so my job at that point was to make sure that my Sponsors were well prepared to explain to the VP why providing sales training should be a top priority and why my company should be the preferred supplier. I'd been asking my Sponsor questions such as "What are the two most important things you want to get out of this initiative?" After getting a reply, I then asked, "Do you think the VP and CLO agree with you?" When he answered "I don't know," I asked if he had any suggestions for trying to find out. This coaching helps make sure my Sponsor has thought through how to best sell my solution to these other members of the Complex Buying Team that I cannot, at this time, get to directly.

The second reason for keeping in touch with the Sponsor after your presentation or proposal is that **even if they decide you are the best choice, it's likely some uncertainty or doubts will surface**. And that's when you need to be prepared to become a Therapist who helps them work through those fears, as I'll discuss in the next chapter.

CHAPTER 8

The Therapist

Understand and Resolve a Buyer's Fears

Tell me if this scenario sounds familiar. You've just reached the end of a great sales presentation, and your prospect says to you, "I'm very impressed with your solution. Call me next week so we can wrap this up. . . ." Chances are you're feeling pretty confident. So you call the next week. No response. You call again. No response. Suddenly you realize that these "sounds of silence" are shouting a message at you—your "sure thing" sale is in serious jeopardy.

Stop and think for a minute about what's going on with your customer. The silent treatment you receive is common because few customers go directly from identifying an ideal solution to making a commitment to buy. It's natural for them to have doubts and concerns that manifest themselves as fear.

The fear associated with buying is obviously not physical terror, but rather a feeling of apprehension, perhaps worry, and often much worse. I remember delivering a workshop where an account manager kept getting up and leaving the room every few minutes throughout the day. I came to learn that one of her customers was having major problems with the installation of her company's product. The second day of the course, this account manager returned from the midmorning break in tears. Her Sponsor inside her client company had just been fired because of the failure of her solution.

This reminded me that when I'm acting in the Therapist mode, I need to think about what the *Fear* step is like from the customer's viewpoint: are they experiencing mild concerns, or is there the lurking fear they could lose their job if everything doesn't work out right? A Power Broker, for example, who has sponsored my solution through the minefield of corporate decisionmaking is now about to put his or her credibility on the line.

The question for us as salespeople is what we can do to help our customers work past these fears so they *will* make the commitment to buy. You shouldn't be surprised to learn that my answer is, "Slow down."

Tip: From "Telling" to "Feeling"

In your previous role as the Coach you analyzed the competition and explained your solution to the customer. Now I'm suggesting that you change your focus to the listening and observing mode of a Therapist— "change your channel" from analytical to emotional intelligence. Become more sensitive to how people function. Consider as well how the buying team, as a whole, functions, and try to anticipate any potential roadblocks at this point.

You must get your mind out of the "telling" mode you were in as a Coach and instead adopt the listening and observing mode of a Therapist. This is one of the biggest shifts in roles that you'll have to make during the buying-focused selling process.

My prescription actually goes a lot farther than "slow down." It has two parts. First, you need to acknowledge that *fear is going to happen*. Second, knowing that you need to expect fear, you can be prepared by including a "fear strategy" in your selling process. What it takes to develop that kind of strategy is the subject of this chapter.

Customer Step 5: *Fear*

In the previous Learn stage of the buying process, the focus of decision makers was on answering the question, "Which option is our best choice?" Their *Comparison* work concluded when a preference was identified. The customer then focuses more intently on that single solution. Now that they are shifting into the Buying phase of the process, their sentiment is "Am I sure I'm about to make the right choice? What happens if I buy product A from company B?"

Note that I didn't say the customer's shift was from "Which choice is best" to "Let's close the deal." That's not how it happens in real life. Most of us will have some anxiety when we're about to make a major decision that has a big impact. Our concerns are not superficial. They may be valid concerns about the consequences of this purchase—or be only indirectly related to the decision.

For example, Sarah was proposing a new PBX phone system to a fairly large regional health clinic. After her presentation, the prospect went silent. When Sarah finally was able to reach her Sponsor by phone, he said the reason for the delay was that the new equipment, in his words, "cost too much." That didn't make sense. Earlier, during her needs analysis, Sarah and the prospect had determined that purchasing a new system that enabled VOIP (Voice over the Internet Protocol) would significantly reduce the clinic's toll charges incurred by ordinary phone service. The expected savings from VOIP would just about match the clinic's monthly lease payment for the new PBX.

Sarah's instincts told her this wasn't an issue to be handled over the telephone. Fortunately, she was successful in setting another appointment, this time face to face. During the meeting, Sarah said, "I get the feeling there's some other concern besides price." And that's when the real reason popped out: the prospect was worried that the new PBX would require significant retraining for remote users (the doctors and medical staff). He was concerned that the powerful physicians might turn against him if there was the slightest difficulty in implementation.

At Sarah's suggestion, she and the prospect visited each remote facility, shared the proposed changes with employees, and brainstormed ways to keep it simple for the physicians. Sarah also helped the office staff recognize all the helpful features that a new system would provide, such as the "automated appointment reminder" capability. The result of these sessions was that the office staff became excited about the new system, communicated their excitement to the physicians, and Sarah's sale went through.

Sarah's success makes the point that the first concern you hear from your prospect is often a smoke screen—even if they tell you they've decided to do nothing.

Recently, my team was involved in a consulting project with a client to design a new sales training program. As part of that project, we contacted thirty prospects who, we were told, had bought from the competition. We discovered that eight of these prospects had *never bought anything*. Eight out of thirty, that's more than 25 percent! Apparently, the prospects had told the salesperson they had bought from the competition just to get the salesperson to go away.

Outright lying to a salesperson isn't unheard of, but more often you might find that a hot prospect suddenly goes silent rather than reveal the cause of their concern. In rare cases, they may actually contact you to say they've changed their minds or postponed the decision.

Tip: Are Lost Sales Really Lost?

Our research finding points out that if you receive the bad news that you've lost a sales opportunity, maybe you didn't. Maybe they've just decided not to buy and don't want the hassle of explaining their decision to you. My suggestion is this: When you lose a sale make a note to call that prospect back six months later. You might find out that they still haven't made a purchase. Perhaps there was another reason they didn't want to explain at the time, but which has now resolved itself. Who knows what might come of calling back?

Why Fear Happens

The one step in the buying process that you may not observe on every sales opportunity is *Fear*. When the customer perceives that the need is urgent enough, and the best choice has been clearly identified, they may move directly from comparing alternatives to making a commitment. When this happens, congratulations! More often than not, however, you will encounter the *Fear* step on your major sales opportunities.

There are eight common fear triggers that can make your customers feel anxious and fearful. Your awareness of these triggers can help you become more effective at anticipating that fear will be a factor, and planning accordingly. The more of these that apply, the greater the likelihood that your customer will experience fear, and the harder you have to work to help them work through this step.

1. **A Major Dollar Investment.** The larger the financial impact of a buying decision, the more likely your prospects will become fearful. A $100,000 decision will cause more concerns than a $1,000 decision.

2. **Reentry of the ROI Authority into the Picture.** As I've discussed before, it's likely that the ROI Authority will disappear in the middle of the decision-making process, only to reappear right about now, when it's time to commit to the purchase. If the ROI Authority didn't attend the various sales presentations, as is often the case, he or she needs to be brought up to speed on the buying team's activities, and perhaps resold on the need for the decision. If significant time has passed since the ROI Authority delegated the investigation part of the decision to the buying team, the team may be concerned about issues such as whether the Authority's priorities have changed, whether he or she will agree with their reasoning, or that he or she will have different criteria than they developed.

3. **Uncertainty About Long-Term Impact.** The greater the future impact of a buyer's decision, the greater the likelihood

they're going to feel fear. A decision to relocate an entire company to a new city would be of more concern than a decision to send key executives to an overseas conference for a few days.

4. **Wrestling with Tradeoffs.** As customers approach D-Day (Decision Day), they have to come to grips with the fact that their learning has uncovered pluses and minuses with every option. The "perfect" solution may not exist. I remember when my wife and I were going to buy a home and had identified two options in the same neighborhood, both with the same exact floor plan and comparable prices. One home backed to a busy street but had a large backyard and nice view. The other home had a lousy view of rooftops but had a pool and no traffic or noise problem. We had to slow down and resolve our concerns about the tradeoffs before we could commit to either option. (We chose the one with the big backyard and nice view but more street noise. As it turned out, the street got even noisier as our town grew, and we ended up moving seven years later.)

5. **A Significant Change in Operations.** The more change caused by the implementation of your solution—and the more people your solution affects—the more difficult the transition's going to be. Also, the broader the impact, the stronger the pressure on decision makers to wonder "Have we gotten all the necessary buy-in for this decision?" (That's what led Sarah's prospect to question the purchase of a new PBX system.)

6. **Having to Face the Reality of Change.** Many decision makers get so wrapped up in making a purchasing decision that they pay little attention to implementation until after they've identified which product they want to buy. Sudden doubts—"What if the changeover takes longer than we anticipate?" "What if we can't function during the transition?" and worst of all, "What if it doesn't work?"—often arise at that time.

7. **Disagreement Among Decision Makers.** During the sales presentation, and immediately after, disagreements between

decision makers can surface due to differences in opinion on what is important, different interpretations of the criteria, and different impressions of the various suppliers who made presentations. The more decision makers who are involved in the sale, the more difficult it is for them to all agree. (If you have been with the decision-making team throughout their buying process, I hope you helped them agree on the definition of the buying criteria. But there may be other sources of disagreement.)

8. **A Radically New Product or Concept.** Chances are the product or service line you sell includes at least one "new idea," a radically different product or concept that most of your prospective customers have never used before. If you're selling a "new idea," your prospects may be reluctant to change—or may doubt that your solution, once implemented, will work properly. New products or concepts require a shift in attitudes, a new way of thinking.

Luckily, most of these scenarios are usually not serious enough to stop the buying process altogether, but they can throw a wrench into your selling strategy. If you *expect* your buyers to experience a certain amount of anxiety, you won't be taken by surprise when they suddenly come up with new objections and seem reluctant to move forward.

When in the *Fear* step, customers will:

- Not return your phone calls.
- Ask questions that may indicate second thoughts about purchasing.
- Raise old concerns that had been previously resolved.
- Send nonverbal signals that all is not right.
- Make unrealistic or inappropriate demands.
- Postpone agreed-upon go-forward commitments.

As I pointed out earlier, occasionally, buyers skip the *Fear* step altogether. However, today most customers have *more* fear about buying, not *less*. For your customers, more technology, more change, and more choice means there's more to learn. And downsizing has forced many C-level executives to delegate buying authority to people in the Core level, people who are closer to the problem that needs to be solved and more knowledgeable about it. But when the *power* to buy is delegated, those with buying authority feel greater pressure to make the right choice. As a result, many salespeople tell me it's taking more time for customers to make up their minds. This is proof that there's increased fear in buying situations.

It is natural for customers to question their decision when it comes time to put money on the table. If you are prepared for this turn of events, customer fears present you with the chance to solidify your position and show again, in another way, why your offering will be valuable.

When the customer slows down, you must do the same. You have to become a Therapist who is skilled at helping the "patient" explore and resolve the uncertainty and doubt that is causing the fear.

How a Therapist Resolves Buying Fears

A Therapist is someone who deals with clients' emotions. They help clients to figure out for themselves what their concerns are—and then help resolve them.

Be forewarned that traditional objection-handling techniques you were taught may not be effective when dealing with fear. You must move from your head to your gut. You must operate on a more intuitive level. Here's an example:

Suppose you are engaged to be married, the wedding is scheduled for next weekend, and you are feeling fearful. Your best friend calls to see how you're doing. Applying a traditional technique would go something like this:

YOU: I'm scared stiff.

FRIEND: Why?

YOU: I'm afraid [*he or she*] is not the right person for me.

FRIEND: Fear is typical for someone about to be married, but keep in mind that marriage has many advantages. Besides, you've already sent out the invitations, your guests have made travel arrangements . . . and your mother is so excited! You will go ahead with it, won't you?

Would your fears be allayed if your friend acted this way? Not likely. Your friend can't help much with this approach because there is no "magic answer" that will make your fear disappear. Also this approach doesn't give you a chance to express your emotions; it moves too quickly past emotion on its way to a logical resolution.

When you encounter a prospect in Step 5, *Fear*, think of what you would say to a close friend. The best way to handle fear is, again, to slow down and take the time to listen to your customer. Encourage open expression of concerns so prospects can move past them.

If your friend knew how to be an effective therapist, he or she might help you through pre-wedding jitters this way:

FRIEND: Can you tell me how you are feeling?

YOU: I'm scared stiff.

FRIEND: Anything in particular that's making you feel afraid?

YOU: I'm afraid [*he or she*] is not the right person for me.

FRIEND: I felt the same way before my wedding. It's perfectly normal to feel afraid. Is there anything I can do to help?

YOU: I guess I'm just totally nervous.

FRIEND: What can you do about it?

YOU: Actually, I'm always nervous before I do something new. Usually, I'm fine once things get started.

Important Skills of a Therapist

When a couple goes to a therapist, the therapist carefully observes the way they interact. What they *do* speaks as loudly as what they *say*. One person may dominate the conversation while the other watches the clock. Not listening, interrupting, sudden slumping in the chair, or reacting with a pained facial expression are all signals—verbal or nonverbal signs—that indicate unrecognized fear or doubts.

That's why the first key to being a good Therapist during the *Fear* step of the sale process is to **be sensitive and observant**. It boils down to your "gut feeling" that something isn't right. Therapists are sensitive to both what is being said and what isn't being said. Something is always happening, even if it's not being discussed. Therapists observe how their patients behave and interact. Therapists have learned that underneath seemingly minor issues are often major problems.

Like a good Therapist, watch for the common signs of fear described earlier in the chapter. If you detect fear in your customer, start by exploring concerns. Be aware that most people have trouble talking about fears directly, and may actually not know themselves *why* they are reluctant to make that final commitment to buy. That's why, when therapists sense repressed emotions, they get a patient to talk about what they are feeling by asking a neutral question: "Can you tell me more about this?" or "What concerns do you have?" If something's not right—but you're unsure what it is— make a good guess. A therapist might say, "I sense that you're reluctant to be here." Therapists tell me that this kind of leading statement, even if the guess is incorrect, often gets the patient to open up.

Your second action is to be empathetic with their clients' concerns. Therapists have learned that helping people realize what their feelings are—and why they are having those feelings—is often all that is required to move forward. **A therapist does not solve a patient's personal problems.** The therapist uncovers, repeats, and restates the client's feelings and thoughts in an effort to help the person gain insight. The goal is for patients to leave therapy knowing what their fears are and what actions they can take to relieve those fears.

Getting the Jump on Fear

No matter how much preparation you do, odds are good that you'll have to deal with customer fears at this point in the buying process. However, you can lessen the effect by proactively dealing with fears before the customer is even aware of them, at a much earlier stage of the sales process.

Lawyers tell me that if they have a weakness in their case, they make sure to bring it up early in the trial or negotiations because doing so leaves plenty of time for the issue to be discussed and dealt with (and takes away an argument from the other side). The same principle is true for making a sale. Basically, if left on their own, your customers may not even recognize their fears until after your presentation, when you're out of the picture. That's why anticipating fear is so important, and why you want to act in advance to prevent fear. If you help your customer to recognize fear while you're still there, you'll have the chance to nip it in the bud.

To be proactive in dealing with fear, you first have to **know the most common purchasing risks experienced by your customers,** the factors that may cause them to feel anxious or fearful at this stage. Figure out what actions you can take or what information you can provide to the customer to resolve their fears.

For example, one of my clients sells point-of-sale technology that integrates with cash registers and makes it easier for sales clerks and cashiers to check stock, research product information, and place specialty orders. The product is primarily sold to small and medium-sized retailers. Among this customer base, there is extremely high turnover in clerks and cashiers, so a common fear is that it will be too hard to have to continually train new staff in how to use the technology. To preempt this fear, my client raises the training issue when prospects are in their *Research* or *Comparison* step. Even more important, my client brings an actual register to sales presentations so that all the decision makers can try the technology themselves and see how easy it is to learn to use.

You can also use knowledge of common fears to draw out your customers. The point-of-sale company could say to prospects: "Some of our customers were concerned about integrating the technologies. Is that a concern for you?" or "Other clients have said that training for cashiers was an issue. Is this a concern for you as well?"

Other options for bringing fears to the surface include:

- When talking with your Sponsor prior to making a presentation or submitting a proposal, ask about concerns.

- Toward the end of your sales presentation, ask: "It's not uncommon at this point to have one or two remaining questions or concerns that I haven't yet addressed. May I ask what possible concerns might you have in regards to implementing a solution such as this?"

Above all, as I stated in Milestone #3, even after you make a presentation or deliver a proposal, you must **stay present in your prospects' lives.** The longer a prospect takes to make a decision, the greater the possibility that fear will develop when you're not there. Therefore, to effectively handle your buyers' fears, you need to talk to them *on a regular basis* to see if uncertainty is growing.

This can be hard to do because now that your customer *thinks* they have all the information they need from you, it's more difficult to reach them. (Have you ever noticed how easily you can get through to customers when they need information—and how impossible they are to reach when they think they know everything?) This is one reason why I always emphasize the need to **request some form of action from your customer**—such as another meeting or phone call—at the end of every contact you make, **and especially at the end of your sales presentation**. This ensures that you get person-to-person time with your prospect just when fear is most likely to become a factor.

Fear May Not be the Only Hurdle

The post-presentation or post-proposal stage of the buying process can be the most frustrating for salespeople. Truth be told, fear is only one reason why a sale can grind to a halt at this stage of a purchasing decision. Other common reasons:

- **A flawed selling process by you.** If you skipped a step, or sold too fast, then the customer may be buying too fast. This is the point when the brakes go on. For example, I commonly see situations where clients have needs that the salesperson did not fully diagnose. Those needs are not fully understood by either the seller or buyer, and therefore the mental picture of an ideal solution can't be fully articulated in a clear and compelling way. The client will likely experience a vague unease that makes them unwilling to commit to the sale.

- **A flawed buying process by your prospect.** We have all had clients whose decision-making processes are a mess. Maybe they aren't sure who should be involved in the purchasing decision. Maybe a control freak ignores input and advice from people who should be part of the decision. Either way, you can do a terrific job of selling and still lose a sale because the client is doing a poor job at buying.

- **Factors outside your control.** In my experience, a sudden silence can happen when something outside of my control has happened inside the prospective client company—a change in budgets, poor quarterly performance, a key decision maker who left (or a new one who enters the picture), a change in corporate priorities, a change in corporate leadership, etc.

You can do something about the first situation—a flawed selling process by you—by following the advice I've given throughout this book. Slow down so you can sell faster: Do your research so you have a good understanding of the client's business before you meet with the prospect. When a customer tells you their first need, help them recognize a second and third need. Dig under every need to diagnose causes; discuss the effects of those problems—and the costs that will be incurred—by *not* fixing them. Participate in the customer's solution design. Present a differentiated solution with unique capabilities that are linked to explicit customer needs.

There is little you can do to recapture a particular sale if you encounter a flawed buying process or factors outside your control, but the following tactics can help:

- If you did a good job of diagnostic questioning in your Doctor role, you should have ample ammunition for **pointing out the cost of delay to your prospect** (what complications they themselves said they'd experience if a change wasn't made soon). Emphasizing the urgency will help if the need for your solution still exists (and is still a priority); it won't do much good if one of the "outside" factors has come into play.

- **Keep in touch with your Sponsor.** Just as factors outside your control can stop one sale, it can open up opportunities for others. Remember the story in Chapter 2 about how I lost a follow-up sale when an unknown factor (the VP of marketing) entered the buying process and shut me out? Well, it turns out that VP was later fired . . . and the company returned to me to provide sales training. I was still in the picture because I'd kept in touch with my Sponsor. In fact, this company became a loyal customer.

Tip: Breaking the Silence

The following situation has happened to all of us. You deliver your presentation, but then your customer "goes silent" on you. Your follow-up phone calls go unreturned, and you have no next-step meeting with the customer scheduled. What can you do? Answer: adopt the role of a Therapist and send a short email, something like:

"Thanks again for taking time recently to evaluate our solution. I get the feeling we've hit some sort of snag on this. Can we talk?"

Any answer is better than no answer.

Resolving Your Own Fears

Customers aren't the only people who start having doubts late in the buying process.

A branch sales manager for a major document services company told me recently that one of his salespeople had proposed a $3 million contract for a potential customer. The customer said they would finish their evaluation within four to five weeks, and would "probably" sign contracts at that point. The manager told me that based on relationships his sales team had developed with the prospect, the completeness of their sales approach, and their ability to answer the prospect's financial concerns, everyone in the branch office was confident they would win, and they would conclude the paperwork within the customer's timeline.

As you can imagine, though, such a large potential account had management's attention throughout the document company. One of the SVPs from the Western Region office was both less confident in the sale and more impatient. He wanted to show the locals that the company could not wait until the "last minute" to close such a big deal. So he phoned the branch sales manager and said he wanted to go to the prospective account and meet someone at a similar executive level the Monday after Thanksgiving.

The sales manager knew that this was a complication that both he and the potential customer did not need. So he politely asked the SVP to review the account plan, the outsourcing study, the proposal, and the internal customer ROI projections. Then he asked the SVP to tell him what new information he (the SVP) could bring to the deal *that would not change the pricing proposal.* The SVP scoffed at the request, but read all the information anyway. He did not call back, and the branch team won the sale in mid-December, just as the customer had said might happen.

If you start fretting over the customer's silence, **reexamine everything you did during the sales process** to, hopefully, remind yourself that you did a good job and the decision is largely out of your hands at this point. If you conducted good discovery sessions, mapped your solution to their needs, differentiated yourself from the competition, and have honest positive feedback from the customer, then you add little value by pestering them with unnecessary calls or emails. If you cut corners in the sales process, or blindly replied to an RFP, then it's probably too late to save the sale anyway. You can try going back to the customer to fill the gaps in the sales process—but the odds aren't good at pulling that off to win the sale.

Help Customers Move Past Fear

Your sale will involve change for your customer—and change involves risk. The greater the risk perceived by your prospect, the greater the probability that fear's going to be a factor.

By assuming the role of Therapist you help your prospects resolve their fears, move past indecision, and arrive at the point of commitment. Now, the negotiations begin.

CHAPTER 9

The Negotiator

Reaching a Mutual Commitment

I believe that we're all born genius negotiators. I know this is true because I'm a parent. Years ago, my son Kyle brought home good grades on his report card. I wanted to reward him. I said, "Kyle, I'm very proud of you, and to show you how happy I am about your grades you can pick one of three options. I'll buy you one video game, two CDs, or I'll take you and a friend to a San Francisco Giants baseball game."

You should have seen the wheels turning inside Kyle's head as he considered my offer. He said, "Dad, let me think it over." A short while later, he came back to me and said, "Dad, I have another idea. How about if you buy me two CDs and just you and I go to the baseball game?"

I knew I'd been had, so I said, "Kyle, let me think it over." Later that day I went back to him and said, "Okay, you win. I'll buy you two CDs and you and I will go to a Giants baseball game." Kyle said, "With a friend?"

I had to admire Kyle's negotiating skills. His instinctive reaction to my offer was to slow down and think it over. And once he thought it over, he came up with a new combination that met both his needs and my needs in a different way. Essentially, he enlarged the pie. (And he nibbled at the end.)

I realize that you're not going to be able to walk away from a negotiation the way that Kyle did, but there are techniques for slowing down the negotiation process, giving yourself precious time to think. Which is a good thing because every sale you make is going to involve some form of negotiation. Customers have learned that when they ask for a better deal, they usually get one. For you, mistakes at this point of the sale can be very costly. So it's time to hone your negotiating skills.

First, keep in mind you should be negotiating at the *end* of the sales process, not the beginning. There's no reason to talk price unless your customer wants to buy. **Never cut your price before buyers recognize what they need and why they need it.** Don't assume that if you lower your price your offering will become more attractive. The reality is that it doesn't matter whether an offering costs five thousand or fifty thousand dollars. If your customer doesn't need it, any price is too high.

The optimal outcome of a negotiation is win-win—the customer is happy with the value they are getting for the money and you are happy with the price you're getting for what you deliver. A mutually beneficial outcome is the goal of a customer-focused negotiator.

Astute readers may have picked up the fact that thus far in this book I have never advised you to "close" the sale. That's because the word "close" denotes an ending, when in fact the end of negotiation is the *opening* of what will hopefully be a long and mutually beneficial relationship. Keeping that "open" mentality in mind will help you negotiate with a win-win attitude.

This chapter examines the most common customer negotiating tactics, and analyzes negotiating power and how you can get more of it! When you apply these ideas in your negotiations you'll make more money, and you'll have happier customers who want to buy more from you.

Customer Step 6: *Commitment*

The customer's sixth step in the buying process is *Commitment*.
Their focus has now changed from determining the
value of your solution to the managing of its cost.
No longer are they wondering, "Why should I buy?
Who's best? What happens if I buy?" Instead, their
focus becomes "How much?" They will:

> Review the specifics of your contract offering.
> Complain that your price is too high.

Negotiations between you and your buyer occur because your
buyer wants a better deal than the one you initially offered. On the
one hand, a buyer wants to buy your product or service On the other
hand, the buyer's interest—a lower price, easier payment terms,
faster delivery, more training, and so on—differ from the terms you
proposed. The actual negotiation process begins when your prospect
presents you with a purchasing request, demand, or condition.
When this moment arrives, you need to be prepared.

How a Negotiator Creates Win-Win

The trouble with our natural negotiating skills is that somewhere
along the line they get either lost or misdirected. I've heard from
many, many sales managers that their reps
spend more time negotiating with *them* than
with the client. The prospect asks for a 25 percent discount and the sales rep says "I'm not
sure I can get that but let me see what I can
do." Then they start negotiating with their
boss without ever offering a counterproposal
to the customer.

To end up in a win-win negotiation, each side has to gain something for each concession they give. The concessions can't be one-sided. Each party should walk away from the negotiations feeling good about the agreement.

The following tips and advice are all aimed at teaching you effective negotiating skills.

Evaluate Your Negotiating Power

In every type of negotiation, negotiating power plays a major role. For each party in a negotiation, power is their perception of their strength or weakness in comparison to the other party's. This perception of power affects the ability of each party to achieve its own goals. **Your negotiating power is largely a reflection of how effectively you've sold up till now.** The more negotiating power you have in comparison to that of your buyer, the fewer *costly* concessions you will have to make.

I'm amazed how many salespeople underestimate their negotiating power. Early in my sales career, I was trying to secure a large office equipment sale to the legal department of one of the world's greatest technology companies. They were taking their time making a decision. Our sales process took four months, and negotiations took place during three separate meetings spread out over two weeks. I was anxious to get the deal done, but all they wanted to do was keep asking me questions about my terms, features, options, etc. They were stringing me along, and it was working. I was feeling pretty frustrated.

That's when my sales manager told me to relax. He said that the customer wouldn't keep talking to me if they didn't want to buy. Keep that thought in mind. It's important: **the customer wouldn't be negotiating with you if they didn't want to buy.** People are busier than ever and nobody has time to waste. If they need to take their time to make a decision, fine. Just be sure to keep the conversation going. And don't leave one appointment without scheduling another.

A quick approach for evaluating your negotiating power prior to a negotiation is to consider the four primary sources of power: need, options, time, and relationships.

Need. The more significant and urgent the customer's need is the more negotiating power you have. Take another look at the MOU you generated. (You did generate an MOU, didn't you?) The MOU should have described the need and the importance to the customer of meeting that need (and/or the impact of *not* solving the problem or taking advantage of the opportunity).

Options. A buyer who believes your offering is identical to those of competing sellers has viable options, which puts you in a weaker negotiating position. The more buying criteria you have uncovered and linked to the strengths of your solution, the greater your negotiating power. This way you make yours the preferred solution.

Together, these two pieces of information, need and options, will give you a general sense of how badly the customer wants to make a change and how strong your position is compared to the alternative solutions they have.

There are two additional sources of negotiating power for you to consider. These are time power and relationships power.

Time. During the sales process you want to listen carefully for any possible time deadlines for a decision. Ask your Sponsor, early on, if there are any particular deadlines for making the decision. If you are a commercial real estate broker, for example, the date that your prospective client's existing office lease expires will affect their timeline for making a decision. Another example is selling to governmental agencies. The nearing of a fiscal year deadline is often an incentive for a government agency to spend (their budgets are often "If you don't use the money this year, you won't get as much next year"). Deadlines put time pressure on your customer and, assuming your solution is their preferred choice, puts you in a stronger negotiating position.

Relationships. There are a few core questions here. How much importance does the prospect place on relationships with suppliers? (If not a lot, then the next questions won't matter.) How strong is your relationship with the prospect? Do you have contact with only one person on the Complex Buying Team, or with several? (You develop negotiating strength in this area by nurturing a high *quantity* of high-*quality* relationships within each prospective account.)

Knowledge Is Power

We all know that knowledge *is* power. You will have more power in the negotiations if you thoroughly understand your customer's problems and needs and can foresee how your solution will make a significant impact on your customer's business. If you have considered the client's needs, have distinguished your solution from the competitors', are aware of any customer timelines or deadlines, and have created strong relationships with your Sponsor(s), then you have a pretty thorough knowledge of what's going on for your customer. All these elements should put you in a strong negotiating position, or at least will give you a more accurate understanding of your negotiating position prior to the negotiation.

Preparing to Negotiate

In preparing to negotiate you need to figure out what you want from the negotiations and how flexible you're willing to be on each of these points. Then, for each item, develop an explanation that justifies the position you desire.

Being prepared to make the right concessions—those that cost you little, but give your customer much—is also key to having the actual negotiations go smoothly.

Here's the worksheet that I use to organize my thoughts prior to any negotiation.

Figure 9-1 Negotiations Preparation Worksheet

Negotiable Area	Initial Terms	Minimum/ Walkaway	Goal/ Target
Price			
Quantity			
Time			
Features			
Service			
(Other)			
Competitive strengths important to this buyer 1. 2. 3. 4.			
High-value, low-cost concessions 1. 2. 3. 4.			

Prep Step #1: Determine Your Flexibility on Negotiables

Most salespeople think of price as the primary focus of negotiations—and indeed it is. However, you also should consider other areas for which to establish negotiating goals. There are, in fact, five common factors that enter into most negotiations:

> Price
> Quantity
> Time
> Features
> Service

For each area, you need to establish your **target goals** and your **range of flexibility**:

Initial Terms: the pricing and terms you communicated in your proposal.

Minimum/ Walkaway: the least you would be willing to accept for each item.

Goal/Target: what you reasonably hope to achieve for each item at the conclusion of negotiations.

A worksheet like that shown in Figure 9-1 can help you think through your various options before conducting your negotiations.

Prep Step #2: Identify Your Competitive Strengths

The first sale you need to make is the one you make to yourself. If you don't believe your offer is reasonable you won't be able to convince anyone else. So in preparing for negotiations, use the work you did in the Architect and Coach roles to develop justifications for the reasonableness of your offer.

Take another look at the competitive assessment worksheet that we saw in Chapter 7 (Table 7-1, page 140). This competitive assessment compared one offering against its two top competitors in terms of the customer's priorities. Assuming that you performed a similar exercise for your sales opportunity, your competitive advantages will already be listed. The competitive analysis should have broken down your offering against your two top competitors. Areas in which your product, service, and/or company are superior or strongly superior are the reasons why the customer should buy from you. Obviously, areas in which you are below average will be a vulnerability or weakness.

From previous chapters, you know that a lot is going on behind the scenes as your prospect discusses options and comes to a decision. You want your Sponsor to be selling your solution to the rest of the buying team. Here, you can use your strengths to explain to your Sponsors—and help them explain to others—why your product or service is the best choice.

Prep Step #3: Identify Your Bargaining Chips (High-Value, Low-Cost Concessions)

Negotiation is always a give-and-take process. You have to have something to give your customer besides a discounted price. The rule is: **Don't walk into a negotiation without at least three concessions (besides price) you can offer.** The best bargaining chips are those concessions that are of high value to your customer, but low cost to you.

How will you know what is of high value to your customers? Once you have fully prepared your negotiating position, competitive strengths, and potential concessions, you should always review the situation from your customer's perspective. This also helps you anticipate the customer's demands. With your customer hat on, ask yourself:

> ➤ "What are my goals?"

> ➤ "What's important to me?"

> ➤ "What concessions could I ask of the seller that I would consider high value?"

Once you've thought through these questions, take off your customer hat and look for bargaining chips that you can use as concessions during your negotiations. Typical "chips" include:

➢ Additional services

➢ Additional options

➢ Training

➢ Product or service customization

➢ Payment schedule adjustments

➢ Future considerations in ordering

As a final step, think about all the concessions you've ever given and identify where they would go in a grid like that shown in Figure 9-2.

Figure 9-2 Value-Cost Matrix

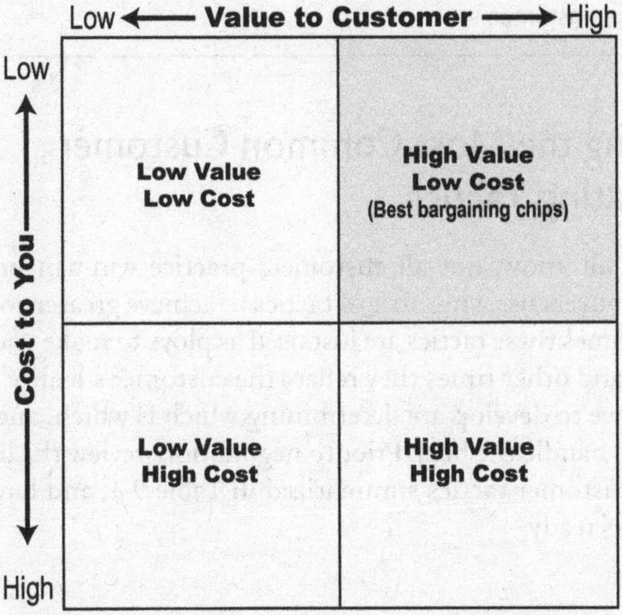

Obviously, your best bargaining chips will be those that are of high value to your customer and low cost to you (*upper* right quadrant). Typically, a price discount would go in the *lower* right quadrant because it costs you just as much to provide it as the value it affords to the customer.

Tip: Using Concessions Effectively

Concessions are an essential negotiating tool, but use them wisely.

- **Consider the future impact of potential concessions.** Today's concession becomes tomorrow's customer expectation. So don't give away the store today or you'll have nothing to give tomorrow.
- **Make sure you get a concession for every one you give.** Instead of saying, "Yes, I can reduce my price by 10 percent," say, "If I can do that, would you be willing to add a third year to the agreement?" Be sure you know what concessions you want from your customer.

Handling the Most Common Customer Negotiating Tactics

As we all know, not all customers practice win-win negotiating. Some buyers use a number of tactics to achieve greater concessions. Sometimes these tactics are just used as ploys to make you feel powerless and other times they reflect the customer's reality. The skills you have to develop are determining which is which, and knowing how to handle the heat. Prior to negotiation, review the list of common customer tactics summarized in Table 9-1, and have your responses ready.

When the Negotiation *Really* Begins

Preparation is important, but it's not everything. You also need to understand how to work effectively during the heat of the moment when you are confronted with a skilled negotiator.

(text continues on page 193)

Table 9-1 Common Customer Negotiating Tactics

TACTIC	EXAMPLE	YOUR OPTIONS
Budget Limitation	"We've only got $10,000. You're going to have to come in under that figure to earn our business."	The issue of budget likely came up back at the beginning when the prospect asked you for a ballpark figure. If the money wasn't in the budget, why have they spent all this time and energy talking to you? Four options here: 1) Extend the budget period (straddle a second payment into next year's budget). 2) Ask about funds from a different budget. If your solution will benefit another department perhaps that department can help pay for it. 3) Take your proposal back and ask the customer about each specific line item, with the intent of removing certain items now deemed less important to meeting the customer's needs. 4) Offer to wait until the next budget period, but remind the customer of their cost of delay. As a Doctor you learned the costs if the customer doesn't change. Now is the time to review these costs from your original MOU.
Other Options (Competition)	"The quote from your competitor is for much less. If you don't lower your price, I'll have to buy from them."	Remind the prospect of your unique strengths and capabilities, then shut up and see what the customer says next.
Foggy Recall	"Didn't you say installation was included in the purchase price? That's what I told the committee. So there's no way I can get any more money."	The best way to handle foggy recall is to prevent it in advance by putting everything in writing, capturing their needs in an MOU, and then your solution in a formal proposal. Don't trust memory, either yours or your customer's, on important terms and conditions! Whenever you discuss terms with the prospect, *immediately* confirm your understanding with an email.

Table 9-1 *(Continued)*

TACTIC	EXAMPLE	YOUR OPTIONS
Good Guy/ Bad Guy	One buyer tells the seller that the sale is a "sure thing," then another buyer gets involved and says there's no way the deal will get approved on the existing terms.	The "other buyer" is often the prospect's home office. Say, "I didn't realize that home office approval was needed. Can we schedule a conference call to get this resolved?"
Wince	When a price is quoted, the buyer winces or acts angry. The buyer may then become silent, waiting to see how the salesperson responds.	Some customers like the wince because they know salespeople hate the uncomfortable silence that immediately follows. To counter, try a reverse wince. When the customer winces immediately ask, "What were you expecting?" Then, whatever their answer is, wince back and say, "Wow. I wasn't expecting to hear that."
Bait and Switch	The buyer requests a price on a large quantity of items, say 100 units. At the last minute, the buyer decides to buy 25 units per year for the next 4 years. Of course, the buyer still expects the 100-unit price, as if all units had been bought at once.	Buyers know full well that it's unrealistic to get the same price over an extended period of time, but they'll often give it a try. You can counter this tactic when you write your sales proposal. Be specific about the terms and limitations of your offer. Additionally you can say, "I didn't realize your needs had changed so much. Allow me to take my proposal back and change it to meet your new needs."
Nibbling	The buyer makes small additional requests, either before or after a deal is done, such as "By the way, if you could give us an extra 5 percent off, it would really help my boss out and it will give you an advantage on our next purchase. What do you say?"	First, isolate it by asking, "Other than 5 percent, is there anything else we need to discuss?" Then ask for a concession in return. Ask, "If I could do that, would you buy a similar quantity next year?" A solid and clear proposal helps here, too.

Specifically, you must understand the guidelines for effective negotiations and conduct your activities in accordance with them—listening for your customer's interests, creating innovative win-win alternatives, and gaining commitment.

The negotiation will begin in earnest when your buyer presents a demand, and it's almost always related to your pricing. The first demand is often an extreme one. At precisely this moment, many salespeople make a big mistake: they immediately react. As human beings, when someone pushes us, our knee-jerk response is to push back. When we push back, we react emotionally in some way. We either confront and "fight it out," or we concede immediately in order to end the conflict. Either way, it's bad for us.

Salespeople need to change their attitude about a buyer's initial demand. Don't confront it, welcome it. Tom Crum, the author of *The Magic of Conflict*, says we need to change how we respond to confrontation. Crum uses the martial art of aikido as a metaphor for handling conflict.[15] The purpose of aikido is to render an attack harmless without harming the attacker. This is the result you want from your sales negotiations.

In aikido, you handle an attack by moving *toward* the source of the attack, not away from it. Think about it. A punch is relatively harmless if your face is two inches away from your attacker. Another example might be how you regain control of your car in a skid. You turn your wheels *toward* the skid, not away from it. You go with the energy, not against it.

When presented with an unrealistic demand in a sales negotiation, don't dig in and fight. Instead, use indirect action, the opposite of what your buyer thinks you'll do (and what you feel like doing). Accept their demand as a positive development. Paraphrase what the customer said, then start asking questions, as discussed in the next section.

Negotiation Guidelines

Here are some guidelines that will help you negotiate solutions that are mutually beneficial to you and your buyer:

- Get a concession for every one you give. Ask, "If I could do that, would you be willing to do this . . .?"
- Consider consequences of concessions.
- Avoid negotiating too early. Don't use a concession early in the sales process as a means of creating buyer interest.
- Avoid negotiating too fast. Slow down and ask questions.
- Avoid confrontation. Acknowledge, then paraphrase your buyer's negotiating demands.

Questions to Ask in a Pricing Negotiation

Chuck sells hospital beds. When one of his prospects told him his price was too high, Chuck responded, "Thanks for mentioning that. How much of a difference are we talking about?" The prospect said, "Yours is 15 percent higher than your competition." Chuck answered, "I can certainly understand your concern. I'm wondering, however, how did you arrive at that 15 percent figure?" The prospect then said, "I compared the price of your model to the price we were quoted for your competitor's Model 2020."

Chuck instantly recognized that the customer wasn't comparing apples with apples. The competitor's surgical bed didn't include a built-in scale or an integrated air surface, a feature that reduces pressure on the patient, which the customer had previously mentioned was important. Once Chuck pointed out these differences to the prospect, it became very clear why Chuck's bed was more expensive. Chuck went on to say, "We have a model that's comparable in price to the competitor's model 2020. Is that more along the lines of what you had in mind?" In the end, Chuck sold the more expensive bed.

As Chuck's example points out, when your buyer presents you with a pricing demand, first learn more about it. This is the essence of win-win negotiating. To offer an alternate solution, you need to understand the reasons behind a customer demand and get something in return.

If a buyer requests a 25 percent discount, there could be several reasons for it. Perhaps a competitor you thought you defeated is back in the game and they offered the customer 25 percent off . . . or maybe the customer's budget just got cut . . . or it could be that this buyer always asks for a 25 percent discount because they frequently get it. "Motive" questions will be helpful. Ask "May I ask how you arrived at that figure?" or "What's the reason for that?" Whatever the motive is, you must address it.

A good rule of thumb is that any time you feel pressure in a negotiation, just start asking questions.

In fact, there's an effective sequence of questions shown below that can help you explore the thinking behind any pricing demands that your customer makes, and achieve a win-win agreement.

Table 9-2 shows you a plan for handling the challenging issue of "your price is too high."

Three Ways to Ask for Commitment

When you're sure all the issues have been resolved, ask for the buyer's business. You've earned their trust, helped with their recognition of needs, and proven that you and your solution are best. Chances are, your buyer is waiting for you to ask for the business, and you certainly don't want to disappoint. Also, if you *don't* ask directly for the business, that may confuse your customer. When you ask for the business, you are also sending the message that you would really like to work with the customer. Here are some non-manipulative ways to ask for the business:

- Ask, "What should be our next step?"
- Give a detailed explanation of what will happen between now and installation, then ask, "Does that sound acceptable to you?"
- Ask, "Is there any reason why we can't go ahead with this proposal?"

Table 9-2 Questions to Ask When Negotiating Price

SEQUENCE OF QUESTIONS TO ASK OF A CUSTOMER	PURPOSE
"So, you feel that our price is out of line. Can you tell me what makes you say that?"	The customer's first demand is often unreasonable and may come as a surprise to you. By repeating it back you achieve two goals: 1. You gain time, perhaps just a few seconds, to think, and, when your customer hears from you exactly what they just demanded, they may recognize it is unreasonable. 2. Asking for more information buys you more time to think.
"Other than price, is there anything else we need to discuss?"	Isolates the demand and prevents the customer from "nibbling," making additional demands after you have made concessions on the first demand.
"How much of a difference are we talking about?"	How far apart are you? What's the number the customer is looking for?
"May I ask, how did you arrive at that number?"	Behind each negotiation request your customer makes is typically an underlying interest, a reason for it. For example, maybe that's the price your competitor quoted, perhaps that is all that's in the customer's budget, or maybe the customer is not comparing apples with apples (as in Chuck's example above). Understanding your customer's interests, needs, and motivations underlying a pricing demand will help you find ways to reach a mutually beneficial agreement faster.
"If I'm able to gain approval to work with you on our per-unit pricing, would you be willing to commit to buy more units?"	Using the phrase "gain approval" suggests some flexibility but limits your authority, which may reduce the pressure on you. The question also asks for a concession from the customer, in this case a larger order, in exchange for a concession from you. Know what concession you want from your customer (e.g., larger sale, longer contract period, etc.) before negotiations begin.
Ask the customer about the continued importance of their specific needs that your solution's strengths are capable of fulfilling. Proceed to ask for commitment.	Confirming that your strengths are still important to the customer allows you to switch the focus of conversation away from price to value.

Negotiate to a Win-Win Agreement

To the well-known words of President John F. Kennedy, who said, "Let us never negotiate out of fear, but let us never fear to negotiate," we would add, "to a win-win agreement."

The essence of "win-win" negotiating is to uncover the underlying reasons beneath your prospect's demand, then propose an alternate solution that addresses those reasons and/or meets the customer somewhere between the two of you. Or, better still, create an alternate, enlarged solution that creates greater value for both you and your customer.

Your goal in selling and negotiating is always to achieve agreements that meet the present and future needs of your customer, your company, and yourself.

Successful agreements must stand the test of time. If you're to keep the customer you have created, the negotiations must strengthen the buyer-seller relationship, not weaken it. Regardless of whether you negotiate with Dr. Jekyll or Mr. Hyde, your approach should always be win-win.

Transitioning from Pre- to Post-Sale

Y ou just got the call. Made the sale. After a little celebrating, what next?

Many salespeople think that their *sales* process is now done, but remember that your customer's *buying process* isn't over. For them, the important part is just beginning.

In his 1986 book *The Marketing Imagination*, Harvard Business School professor and marketing guru Theodore Levitt wrote that the relationship between buyer and seller doesn't end when the sale is made. "The sale merely consummates the courtship. Then the marriage begins. How good the marriage is depends on how well the relationship is managed by the seller. That determines whether there will be continued or expanded business, or troubles and divorce. . . ."[16]

You and your company are in a period of transition, from trying to win the sale to trying to win the customer's loyalty.

Is customer loyalty really important? You be the judge: I recently spoke with the CEO of a Fortune 500 company. He told me that his company could increase sales 40 percent each year for the next five years without a single new customer, *if* they could develop more long-term consultative relationships with customers.

In their most recent report, HR Chally interviewed over 2,500 customers and collected their opinions of more than 4,000 individual salespeople. Chally found that the number-one need customers have in a salesperson is for that salesperson to "be personally accountable for our desired results."[17] To be sure, there were additional needs customers have—needs similar to those already discussed in this book, like understanding the customer's business, solving customer problems, and designing the right applications. But all of these additional needs will be accomplished by you if you hold yourself personally accountable for the desired results of your customers. This, then, is the "cornerstone" commitment required by you for creating customer loyalty.

Do You Keep or Hand Off Implementation?

Exactly what you are personally accountable for will vary depending on how your company is structured to handle post-sales support and relationship development. I typically see three scenarios:

1. **The salesperson hands off implementation support to another individual or team, but then reassumes responsibility for growing the account once implementation is complete.** The salesperson is still responsible for the customer's satisfaction but is not down in the weeds of the implementation/training, instead acting more like a "chairman of the board" who provides periodic oversight and direction. The salesperson pursues other sales opportunities while the new customer's solution is being implemented, then reassumes the account after installation, and grows the relationship from there.

2. **The salesperson hands off all responsibility to an account manager** who oversees implementation, is responsible for customer satisfaction, and looks for opportunities to grow the account further. Meanwhile the salesperson

who created the new customer moves on to pursue other sales opportunities.

3. **The salesperson maintains responsibility for the customer post-sale.** He or she manages the implementation, continues providing support for the customer, and looks for opportunities to grow the account further.

No matter which model your company uses, it is clearly your responsibility to make sure that the transition from pre- to post-sale goes smoothly. If you are not personally providing the post-sales support and relationship building, hand this book to the person who is!

Drafting an Implementation Plan

Immediately after a customer signs on the dotted line they have two types of expectations. First, they expect to see you putting together, with your team and theirs, a detailed implementation plan. Second, the customers have expectations of value that will be achieved by your solution. The following two chapters, "The Teacher" and "The Farmer," describe your responsibilities for achieving customer value based on their expectations. In this transition phase, however, you need to create a draft implementation plan.

The word "draft" is key here. While the customer wants to see evidence that you've put in the effort to design the implementation, **they will not *own* the implementation or the results unless they are involved in shaping that plan.** Still, it will speed up the process if you come in with a draft.

Your draft plan should reflect your best effort at identifying actions, timelines, and responsibilities given your understanding of the customer's business. But in the next step, you will collaborate with the customer on refining the plan.

Minimizing Customer Risk

Earlier, during the *Fear* step, your customer had doubts and concerns regarding the likelihood of achieving results. Through your effective adoption of the Therapist role you were successful at handling those concerns, resulting in a sale. But each perceived risk, from the customer's perspective, is related in some way to uncertainty: "Will we achieve the results expected? What will my boss and others think about this decision?"

Customer uncertainty about those risks and fears still lurk under the surface. They will be watching your implementation like a hawk to see if you and your company will stand and deliver on what you promised. **Now you must diminish customer risk by driving up value achieved**, which is what you do in your next sales role, that of Teacher.

CHAPTER 10

The Teacher

Teach Customers to Achieve Maximum Value

I n Chapter 1 I described my meetings with three different financial planners as each of them attempted to persuade me to choose his investment advisory firm. Each was extremely effective at building rapport, making me feel comfortable, and creating a perception of caring—so much so that "relationship" became a non-factor in my decision because all three seemed to care.

I suspect the same is true for most customers today. The perception that a salesperson cares about the customer is not nearly as important a factor in making the initial decision as it used to be, because most salespeople can give that impression (even if they don't mean it).

However, caring *is* still a critical factor when it comes to converting a new customer into a loyal customer. Nowadays, the customer begins to get a sense whether or not the salesperson really does care *soon after the contract is signed*. They will learn what was more important to the salesperson all along—the customer or the commission?

The *Expectations of Value* step is, then, the precise point in the buying process when you *can* truly differentiate yourself by caring about your customer. Providing strong and consistent support for your customer *after* your solution has been delivered is the single most important thing you can do to maintain a good relationship and generate repeat business.

The secret is to get closer to your customers, not just during the sales process, but after it. The days of hit-and-run selling—closing the sale and moving on—should be over.

To maximize your sales potential, you must work hard at creating satisfied customers. By defining and shaping your customers' expectations, you create a benchmark against which your customers can measure success. Also, you "freeze" your customers' expectations, at least for a while, and prevent those expectations from rising. Finally, you give yourself and your teammates a specific goal to shoot for.

When you apply the first six sales consulting roles described in previous chapters, you'll be well on your way to *creating* more customers. This chapter and the next—the Teacher and the Farmer—will help you become more effective at *keeping* customers.

Customer Step 7: *Expectations of Value*

Here in the last phase of buying, customers are paying attention to the value that they are getting from their recent purchase. An unsatisfied customer is one whose expectations are not met. Unhappy customers have excellent memories. They won't buy from you again, and they tell others of their unhappiness. Not a pleasant scenario.

Some dissatisfied customers are just cranky and impossible to please (born that way?), but many are otherwise reasonable people. What causes a customer to turn on you? Feelings of being unappreciated, let down, or even betrayed. Unhappy customers are often created by salespeople who are unaware of their customers' expectations.

Suppose you sell advertising space and your customer's expectation is that by running a full-page ad in your monthly publication over the next twelve issues their sales will increase by at least 10 percent. Is this a realistic expectation? If six months down the road the customer's sales haven't gone up, does that mean your advertising campaign was a failure? Of course not, because there are so many other factors besides advertising that affect sales, all of which are outside your control (including economic conditions, competition, new products, pricing, management decisions and practices, personnel changes, product quality, sales training). So even if the client's sales *do* rise 10 percent while your schedule of ads is running, how is your customer going to know that the advertising is responsible? The fact is that your client won't know—and neither will you.

Post-purchase, customers will often have a mix of expectations, some directly correlated with the capabilities of your product or service, and some that go far beyond the original needs you helped identify. You have to get your customers to talk about their expectations so you can clearly understand their definition of success. If the expectations are realistic, then you will have a more concrete sense of how you will be evaluated. If the expectations are unrealistic, you have to help the customer dial it down. Otherwise, you will be sacrificing customer satisfaction and loyalty to expectations that are beyond your control.

Lessons from the Learning Curve

Think back to when you were first learning to drive. I'll bet that, like me, before you got behind the wheel, you thought it looked easy. Right? We were, in the language of education, **unconsciously incompetent**—we didn't know that we didn't know how to drive. The dominant emotion was excitement.

For me, that all changed when my dad took me out to the local high school parking lot and I got behind the wheel of his five-speed manual transmission car. Fifteen minutes later, I had killed the engine twice, there was a pungent odor of clutch smoke, and my dad was yelling at me. I was now **consciously incompetent**—I knew that I didn't know much about driving! My confidence and morale plummeted. I was feeling frustrated and angry.

Over the next six months, every time I drove I had my parents or an instructor beside me. When I turned sixteen I arrived at the Department of Motor Vehicles to take my first driver's test. By that time, I was **consciously competent**. I knew much more about driving, but it took my full concentration. I was thrilled by the positive results I saw from my hard work: I no longer stalled out the car, and could actually drive from Point A to Point B without getting in an accident or causing a traffic jam. By then, I was feeling a sense of relief.

Eventually, as with all of us, good driving became something I could do automatically. I became **unconsciously competent.** I could drive and carry on a conversation at the same time.

This same kind of learning curve happens with your customers when you install a new product and/or launch a new service. How quickly they move through this learning curve will vary, depending on how much change your solution requires as well as how good a job you do teaching them how to use it. Left to their own devices, customers may get stranded in the *consciously incompetent* stage, and come away with a sour feeling about you, your company, and your products/services.

Learning is hard work and there is a natural sense of frustration in change and the extra time necessary to learn something new. **The purpose of the Teacher role is to help your customer through their learning curve and, most importantly, through the *conscious incompetent* stage, where that frustration is dominant.**

Your customer's sophistication also plays a role in the severity of their learning curve. Inexperienced customers tend to underestimate the difficulties of change and have unrealistic expectations (often the fault of the salesperson). With all customers, you must walk a tightrope. On the one hand, you don't want to say something that will frighten them and perhaps cost you your sale. On the other hand, you must be honest about what typically happens (good and bad) once your product or service is implemented. This is where post-sale selling techniques are important. Immediately after the sale, you must show your buyers how to make the most of your offering so that their experience will be positive.

The objective, for both you and your customer, is to eliminate surprises and disappointment. Becoming a Teacher, as I'll discuss next, will allow you to:

> Help your customers identify what they expect to *see* after their purchase.

> Help them set realistic expectations.

> Determine measurements of success.

Tip: Who Needs to Be Taught?

For many of us, this step of the buying process brings with it another kind of change: we are no longer dealing with members of the Complex Buying Team (the people who made the purchasing decision), but rather with new people not involved in the purchasing decision. While there may have been one or more representative Users (capital "U") on the buying team, there are likely many, many more users (in the general sense) who will now be involved in implementation.

What you won't know at first is the attitudes of the users toward your solution. If it represents a major shift in job duties or even potential job losses, obviously they will feel threatened. In other cases, they may be eager to see that something is being done to fix the problems or challenges they face every day. You must determine where these people fall on the support/resistance spectrum and explore what it will take for *them* to be successful once your solution is implemented. Consider those factors when developing the final implementation plan.

In short, for your solution to be a success, you need to take into consideration not only the learning curve of your buyers, but also the experiences of whoever will be using your product or service. You must show those who use your product or service how it benefits them personally, and take pains to help them through the learning curve quickly. That is one of the best ways to ensure customer satisfaction.

How an Effective Teacher Instructs Customers: The Four Steps of Customer Education

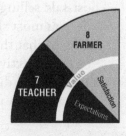

If you think about the best teachers you've had, I'm willing to bet they were good at facilitating your learning process. They didn't rush.

They helped you find your own answers so you were really learning, not just repeating what they said. Think of how your best teachers helped you learn as you work through the steps below.

In the sales role of a Teacher, your activities consist of four steps:

1. Setting realistic customer expectations. Help your customer define exactly what target they're trying to achieve—making sure it's attainable.

2. Refining the draft implementation plan you presented to the customer.

3. Showing customers how to use your product or service.

4. Testing to measure progress. Find out from your customers how they value your solution. All successful salespeople are concerned with results achieved by the customer.

Step #1: Set Realistic Customer Expectations with the Magic Questions

If you've done a good job with the previous sales roles, you should have an idea of what your customer expects from your solution. Presumably, they chose your solution because it best met their needs and buying criteria. Buying criteria now evolve into customer expectations.

However, as noted above, buyers often develop additional expectations that may be subconscious, intangible, vague, and undefined—and worst, perhaps unrealistic.

The danger is that intangible expectations cannot be measured, and may lead to buyer's remorse. You don't want that to happen because unhappy customers don't make repeat purchases.

For example, a customer may be buying a "call center management" service to "improve customer service" (whatever that means) and is privately hoping that sales will increase by 10 percent. For both the customer and the seller to know if the solution has delivered on its promise, they have to know how they will judge whether customer service has improved (perhaps they could measure response and turnaround time) and agree on just how closely they could tie sales figures to better call center management.

If you want to protect against losing your most profitable relationships, you must help your customers identify realistic and observable indicators of your solution's value. If you don't, you're linking your personal success with dozens of factors that are totally out of your control.

The way I like to help set realistic, tangible expectations is by asking **three magic questions**:

1. How will you measure the success of this solution?
2. Six months from today, how will you know this solution is a success?
3. What things will be happening when the value you expect is achieved?

The answers you get will be your customers' expectations of value. Then, based on their answers, determine if it's possible to achieve what they want. If so, great! If not, then it's your responsibility to transform vague or unrealistic expectations to specific and tangible outcomes, much as you do when you help customers define intangible buying criteria in more tangible terms, as you do in your role as Architect (see Chapter 6).

Your objective in asking these questions is to get your new customers to tell you how they will *notice* whether your product or service is a success. If you sell securities and financial services, your client may respond, "The value of my account should increase equal to or better than the S&P 500 index." That response captures the customer's expectations of value, and tells you what observable indicators of value they will be watching.

Step #2: Work with Your Customer to Refine the Implementation Plan

Remember, as I said in Chapter 9, the purpose of your draft implementation plan was to provide a starting point for developing a better plan in collaboration with the customer. The process of refining the draft begins by writing the expectations you and the customer developed at the top of a page, and then seeing how the draft you came in with can be improved to make sure the goals and expectations are achieved. Doing this refinement in collaboration is important because you want the customer to *own* the implementation plan and feel responsible for seeing it be successful. That will not happen if you impose your plan on the customer.

Also, if there is a problem after implementation, you likely won't be present. If it was all *your* plan, you will get blamed if there are delays or other problems. If the customer already has ownership of the plan and was guided by you in developing checklists for troubleshooting, chances are they will just solve the problem themselves.

Step #3: Show, Then Help to Do

I recently took delivery on a new big screen TV. The installer set it up and spent ten minutes showing me everything this miraculous TV could do. Then he left, and I tried to do those same things myself . . . and couldn't do any of them. So I ended up going back to the store. I went into showroom and asked a salesperson to please show me how to use this TV I'd just bought. The salesperson handed me the remote control and walked me through all the basic commands. I went home feeling much more competent.

The original installer made two critical mistakes: (1) he told me a lot of stuff I didn't need to know at the time, and (2) he only *showed* me how it worked, he didn't have me do it myself. This kind of personal experience reminds me to make sure I help my customers apply what I'm teaching (for my line of work, that means using role-playing in our training courses so participants can practice the skills). I urge you to do the same.

When a customer is in the *Expectations of Value* step, it is our job to make sure that they reach the "conscious competence" stage. To help make this happen:

- **Don't try to teach too much in any single session.** Focus first on the customer's most pressing needs. Allow them time to learn and then come back for further lessons. Again, slow down.

- **Create a cheat sheet.** I've never known a customer (including myself) who read an instruction book before trying to use a product or service. That happens in part because most instruction books provide far too much information for the average user. To help your user immediately be able to use your product or service, type up a single sheet of paper with very precise instructions on how to perform the three or four most important things that this customer needs to do. Give them the sheet and have them try those tasks while you observe.

Step #4: Test to Measure Progress

The fourth step in the teaching process is to measure your customer's progress, based on their answer to the first magic question ("How will you measure the success of the solution?") that you will have asked them days or weeks prior. Testing provides important feedback for both you and your customers, helping to acknowledge progress and pointing out areas where the customer still needs your help.

How you test for value depends on the complexity of your sales process, and the complexity of your product or service. For salespeople selling smaller-ticket items, testing for value may be a simple follow-up phone call two weeks after delivery. For those selling multimillion-dollar solutions, testing for value may involve months of tracking, analysis, and reporting.

Regardless of what you sell, it is in your best interest (as well as your customer's) to gain some understanding of your solution's value. The advertising company mentioned earlier might, for instance, look for patterns in the number of phone responses or website hits that are related to a specific advertising campaign.

Another effective way to measure your value is by sending out a survey or questionnaire several months after your solution has been implemented. Include in the survey opportunities for your customer to rate the various elements, features, functions, etc., of your solution.

Also document the lessons they have learned and questions that still remain or issues they would like help with. Salespeople are often surprised when they learn which capabilities of their product or service customers actually use—and what capabilities customers don't use. A clear understanding of how customers benefit can help you become more effective at communicating those benefits to new prospects.

Better still, sit down with your client's implementation project manager and collaborate on developing the questions for your post-implementation questionnaire. That way you can be sure that you are measuring results that are important to the client. Usually, the project manager will then disseminate the questionnaire, collect responses, tabulate the results, then report back to you to discuss next steps. This is a good way to stay involved in your customers' lives.

Teaching Benefits You, the Teacher

If you can't sell your value, you have no choice but to sell by offering the lowest price. To sell your value, you have to understand how much your solution benefits the customer. Following the four teaching steps will help you quantify the value you offer. **Equally important, it will arm you with ROI information that will give you a reason to reconnect with the ROI Authority (the person most interested in return for the investment).** If you don't measure results, you won't have that opportunity.

In addition, learning how to help customers achieve and measure value will help you:

- **Find new sales opportunities.** When you measure the impact of your solution, you may uncover new customer needs to be met. These needs can lead to further sales. Additional purchases will require less deliberation by customers, because you have already proven yourself. Happy customers buy faster.
- **Discover "best practices."** When you measure your value, you find out how your product or service is being used. You'll be amazed at the extent to which some buyers get more value

out of it than others! Once you identify best practices, you can share them with other customers. Your customers' usage—and, therefore, their return on investment—will increase.

Exceed Your Customers' Expectations

Successful salespeople have a common focus. Customers! If you don't satisfy your customers, your competition will. As a Teacher in sales, you help your customer implement your solution in such a way that ensures maximum value. When you commit yourself to exceeding your customer expectations, you place service above self and contribute to the success of others.

CHAPTER 11

The Farmer

Cultivate Customer Satisfaction and Loyalty

M any years ago, when I was a district manager for Lanier, we sold and installed the same centralized dictation system at two different hospitals. At Hospital A, the installation went flawlessly, and our system was up and running in no time. No problems whatsoever. No complaints.

At Hospital B, we went through hell immediately after the installation. A bug in our software was exposed by heavy usage, resulting in lost patient records, frustrated doctors, and very angry hospital administrators. We immediately threw every resource we had at the problem. Our technicians and office personnel worked feverishly to resolve the situation. Finally, we succeeded—the problems at Hospital B were corrected. The difficult times we shared with Hospital B had bonded us together. My team had been tested. The customer saw how much we cared. Over the subsequent months and years, we kept in close touch with this account.

Would you be surprised to learn that Hospital A, our "satisfied customer," called us a few years after we installed their system to tell us that they'd just purchased a new system from one of our competitors? They hadn't even bothered to look at our newest offering! Yet Hospital B, the originally dissatisfied customer, remained a loyal Lanier customer for at least fifteen years.

Obviously, we'd been complacent with Hospital A. We were satisfied with what we had delivered to them—but they weren't satisfied with our care and support. We didn't make them feel important. **Always remember that satisfaction with your solution doesn't automatically translate into loyalty.** You must sow customer satisfaction, much like a Farmer, in order to reap the harvest.

This chapter will teach you how to increase the odds that a customer will shift from "satisfied" to "loyal."

The Key to Customer Satisfaction

The key to customer satisfaction isn't just what you deliver but how you deliver it. Service, support, and frequent customer contact after the sale are all important factors. Meeting your customer's initial expectations isn't enough, however. They want personal acknowledgment from you after the sale. They want you to make them feel important. They want to know you care.

> ### Tip: Keeping in Touch
>
> In Chapter 4 I talked about InsideView.com, which notifies you about significant events within your client companies. Use those events to trigger communication (emails, handwritten notes, phone calls).

In the eighth and final step in the customer's buying process, *Satisfaction*, and its matching sales role, the Farmer, you have two goals. You want to:

1. Make sure the customer has solved their immediate problem or has capitalized on the immediate opportunity. That is one way they will become satisfied with their purchase.

2. Turn satisfaction into loyalty. Your customer may (or may not) be looking to establish a relationship with a reliable vendor. Regardless, your goal is to turn a satisfied customer into a loyal customer, one that will purchase again from you with little hesitation and will recommend you to others.

This chapter looks at satisfaction and loyalty from the customer's perspective. It also describes the keys to staying closer to your customers over the long haul, and shows you what kinds of relationships to seek with different customers. This focus will help you increase repeat sales and enhance customer loyalty.

Customer Step 8: *Satisfaction*

In the *Satisfaction* step, the customer's level of satisfaction is based on how they feel about the following four questions:

1. Am I achieving the results I expected?
2. Is the product or service performing as expected?
3. Did I pay a fair price?
4. Does the way I'm treated by your support people make me feel important?

The first three questions reflect tangible results the customer is expecting from their purchase. The last is more intangible and reflects *how well* you're doing with post-sales support.

If the customer feels confident that the answer to each question is "yes," then you've achieved customer satisfaction (at least for now). But be forewarned: Satisfied customers may not stay that way. Most people are satisfied with a new car for several years . . . until they start noticing newer models on the road with better designs and innovative features. Or perhaps until their life circumstances change and their current car is too small, or too big, or doesn't perform well in certain conditions.

The same thing happens with your customers. Their *immediate* goal after the sale is achieving satisfaction with that purchase. But their satisfaction will change as their business changes or they become aware of new alternatives. If you stay in touch with that customer and keep track of changes, you will find opportunities for additional sales.

Look at the situation from the customer's viewpoint. Once the immediate problem or opportunity is achieved, they face a choice: Do they continue to give *you* access to them and their company or not? The basis of that choice is whether contact with you continues to add value to them.

Say you sell air compressors. You install a new product and teach the customer how to get the most out of it. You believe the customer will need more air compressors in the future, so naturally you want to keep in touch with them. The customer could be perfectly happy with the compressor but if they believe they are already getting everything they can from the equipment and have no immediate plans to buy another compressor, they could shut you out. On the other hand, if you can show them ways to continually lower their cost of ownership by showing them new best practices you've identified, they are more likely to welcome continued contact—and to give you an edge on future sales opportunities.

To turn a satisfied customer into a loyal customer, you have to keep asking yourself, "What value do I continue to bring to this customer? Am I helping them think differently?"

How a Farmer Cultivates Customer Loyalty

Achieving customer satisfaction—satisfaction with your solution's price, performance, and service responsiveness—is the prerequisite for developing any long-term relationship with a customer, and especially one that you may want to take to a higher level of mutual commitment and loyalty.

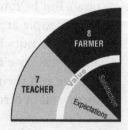

Because your customers' expectations are always on the rise, you've got to stay close to ensure their continued satisfaction. **Becoming complacent because your customers have made their purchase is the number-one killer of customer satisfaction.** Complacency is a feeling of satisfaction in the mind of the salesperson, but not necessarily in the mind of the customer.

The constant attention and nurturing of the customer is why I think of the salesperson's role at this stage as that of a Farmer, and use the term "cultivate" to describe how to achieve loyalty.

True farmers must learn to deal with the unpredictable: torrential rains, sudden freezes, an infestation of bugs, etc. The pests *you* battle are your hungry competitors. You'll find them buzzing around your key accounts. If they're successful at infesting one of your major accounts, they'll savor a double victory—a big win for themselves and a big loss for you. If you want to control these pests and hold on to key accounts, keep close to your customers over the long haul.

Four Keys to Sales Farming

Staying close to customers isn't easy to do because everyone is getting busier. Customers are being forced to do more with less. Busy customers have limited time, and without any urgent business reason to meet with you they may become uncommunicative. You are no longer on their mind, so it's easier for them to drift away.

Here are four simple actions you can take to cultivate greater customer satisfaction and repeat business.

Key #1: Cultivate Your Relationships

Your best asset isn't the client company; it's your personal relationships with the people who buy from you. People buy from people they like. As Dale Carnegie suggested in his classic book, *How to Win Friends and Influence People*, you've got to become genuinely interested in other people. Smile more. Be a good listener. Encourage others to talk. Talk in terms of the other person's interests.[18]

Key #2: Conduct Regular Account Reviews

Farmers regularly run tests on their soil to identify harmful viruses or fungi before it's too late. You should conduct account reviews to test your customers' perception of value and to spot early indications of dissatisfaction. If you think customers are happy just because they haven't complained, think again. Today's customer would rather switch than fight. Problems that are either undetected or ignored can destroy a profitable relationship. Because customers' expectations are always increasing, one follow-up account review is not enough.

What to ask in these reviews? For the purpose of getting an overall sense of how you're doing, follow the advice of Frederick Reichheld, author of *The Ultimate Question: Driving Good Profits and True Growth*. When researching customer loyalty, Reichheld found that only one question had a statistical correlation with the likelihood of future customer purchases when answered affirmatively: "How likely is it that you will recommend us to a colleague or friend?"[19]

But predicting the potential for additional purchases is only just that, predicting. You can discover information that will help in future sales and improve your current customer's experience by asking questions such as:

> What do you like best about our service?
> How would you like to see our service improved?
> Is there any way we can work together better?
> What are your expectations?
> How have your goals changed since the last time we met?

Tip: Ask the "One to Ten" Rating Question

To get a quick impression of how you're doing, ask the customer, "On a scale of one to ten with ten being great, how would you rank our solution?" Whatever the answer is, ask, "What would it take to get to a ten?"

> ➢ What more can we do to help you achieve those goals?
> ➢ Why did you buy from me?

Key #3: Get Specific Answers to Questions About Satisfaction

Treat any vague response as an early warning signal. Remember, many unsatisfied customers would rather flee than fight. Complaining takes time and complaints are often ignored, so customers think, "Why bother?"

Customers often hide their unhappiness by responding to a salesperson's questions in a nonspecific way. You've probably done the same thing in other circumstances. Suppose you dine out at an expensive restaurant, but receive poor service. After your meal, your server asks you, "How was everything?" If you choose to avoid the hassle of complaining, you'll reply with a nonspecific "fine." Only by asking more questions and seeking specific answers might the server learn the real story—the salads arrived too late, the vegetables were overcooked, and the meat was tough. To discover what your customers truly think of your solution, seek specific answers to your questions.

Key #4: Make a Second Sale; Create Greater Customer Attachment

Stockbrokers and banks know that a client who has a single account is more likely to switch providers than a client who has multiple accounts. The more products and services a customer buys from you, the higher their switching costs and the more difficult it is for them to change suppliers. Banks, for instance, strive to sell you a variety of services—checking, savings, credit cards, mutual funds, computer access, and so on—partly because the more services you buy, the greater the hassle for you to change banks.

The same principle holds true for all the salespeople I've worked with. They need to diversify their risk by increasing the customer's attachment to their company. This principle works *as long as those additional products and services increase benefit to the customer.* As you continue to add value by implementing multiple solutions, you become a more valuable supplier for your customers—either because what you sold them second is integrated into what you sold them first, or because the knowledge they continue to gain about their needs and opportunities helps them add more value.

The Three Levels of Customer Relationships

Farmers quickly learn where their investment of time and resources will have the best crop yields. Depending on the nature of your business, you may have opportunities to develop deeper relationships that will yield even more results, or you may have to be content with just selling your product or service and stopping at that. There are three levels of relationships, as shown in Figure 11-1:

Figure 11-1 Levels of Customer-Supplier Relationships

➣ **Approved Vendor.** As an Approved Vendor, you are a viable option when customers recognize future needs. Your price and service are acceptable. At this relationship level, the customer interacts with you for the sole purpose of acquiring a specific product or service at a competitive price. The customer's motivation is utilitarian and event-driven. Once that purchase is completed, the customer's decision makers move on to the next priority.

> **Valued Consultant.** As a Valued Consultant, you provide consulting advice because you are perceived as the "go-to" person. Your expertise regarding a variety of potential solutions is both valued and sought-after when a customer need arises. You understand your customer's business processes and their preferences (many were buying criteria you identified previously). You understand how your solution is currently interacting within the customer's business.

> **Strategic Partner.** As a Strategic Partner, you do more than understand the customer's needs, you *anticipate* them. You provoke new thought for your customer. You help your customer to see the future faster, and in a new and different way. You continually strive to add greater value to your solution and the customer senses that by partnering with you they will achieve continuous improvement of your solution. This is one of the great payoffs for customers who develop strategic partners—**the solution you sold them gets better.** Customer loyalty is extremely high among strategic partners.

For the salesperson, there are two important consequences when dealing with these types of relationships. The first, as shown in Figure 11-2, is the level of access you gain by moving up the pyramid. If you can maintain a relationship with someone at the C-level,

Figure 11-2 Access Levels of Vendor Types

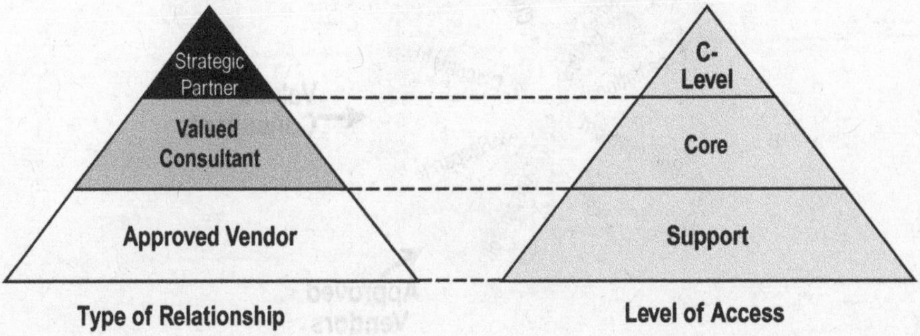

Type of Relationship   Level of Access

it is likely you will be considered a Strategic Partner. (And vice versa, if you become a Strategic Partner, you're more likely to gain broader access to the C-level.) If you are solving operational types of problems, you will likely have direct access only at the Core level. If the customer views your offering as a commodity, then the only issue will be price and your contact will be at the Support level.

Even if you make your first sale at the C-level or Core level, it is likely the customer will want to move you down a level (or two) once you have solved the immediate need. Moving down diminishes the size, number, and nature of opportunities—as well as your ability to influence how the customer defines their needs and buying criteria. It pays to work hard to maintain access to the highest level possible.

The second consequence, shown in Figure 11-3, is that different types of suppliers are brought into the picture in different steps of the buying process.

> Approved Vendors typically don't learn of future sales opportunities until the *Comparison* step, generally after the need has been identified and the buying criteria have been developed. That's because the customer perceives they have the internal expertise to handle the *Discontent* and *Research*

Figure 11-3 When You Learn of New Sales Opportunities

steps on their own. If you enter the process this late, you will have little opportunity to shape the customer's needs or ideal solution. Customer loyalty to Approved Vendors is low, but can be improved provided your service and support is (a) exceptional and (b) important to the successful operation of the customer's business.

➢ Valued Consultants are often brought in during the *Research* step, *after* a need has been identified. The customer will use a valued consultant to "test the feasibility" of their thinking. Generally, your first step should be backwards to reexamine the customer's *Discontent* and needs. Customer loyalty to Valued Consultants is moderate. It can be enhanced, as mentioned in the previous chapter, by testing to measure the value the client achieved with your solution, and then sharing your findings with key customer stakeholders.

➢ Strategic Partners are always present during the lengthy *Change* step. They often see customers' needs before the customer does. These are the steps of the buying process (*Change* and *Discontent*) where the *size* of the customer's need/purchase is determined. By helping a customer to see the entire need and the strategic impact of their choices, the result is often a much larger sale.

The choice of which level of relationship you have will be up to your customer. You can influence the choice, but ultimately it is their decision how far to let you in. If the intensity of the customer need is high, and they recognize your expertise at providing continual and increasing value over time, you may have the *opportunity* to become a partner.

One of my clients, for example, sells outsourced supply chain services, managing logistics for companies who either don't want to do it themselves or for whom outsourcing of logistics is more effective. This client uses sophisticated labor management software to manage *and continually improve* the productivity of employees who provide the warehousing services to their customers. Customers who perceive my client as a value-added supplier now also see that they offer the potential of *getting better over time*—and hence making a long-term strategic partner relationship seem more attractive.

When and How to Develop a Strategic Partnership

You cannot attempt to be a Strategic Partner to every large customer in your territory. It would take too much time. Here are some guidelines for making the decision on whether or not to strive for a Strategic Partner relationship.

The most important piece of advice I can give is not to try to push the role of Partner too soon in your relationship. When a salesperson shares with a customer a desire to "partner" *before* they have fully demonstrated that they can be a "Valued Consultant," it's like wanting to get married on the first date. ***Never* tell the customer that you want to become a partner. The best way to become a partner is to just act like one,** not state it as some self-focused goal or objective that you want to achieve.

Consider the reverse scenario. When a customer tells you during the early stages of a relationship that they want to "partner" with you, what they're really saying is that they want your biggest possible discount. Right?

If you determine that it is the right time to pursue partnerships, think about the Pareto principle, which reflects the fact that you likely get 80 percent of your sales from 20 percent of your customers. Is the account you want to partner with among that productive 20 percent? If not, they may not be worth your effort.

Another application of the Pareto principle is to apply the 80/20 rule to profitability instead of sales revenue. Who are the 20 percent of customers that generate 80 percent of your profits? Some companies realize that a customer generating a high sales revenue may require so much energy—or have such a steep discount—that they are actually less profitable.

Besides sales and profit potential, here are some additional factors to consider:

> The amount of additional value you can provide your customers over time. Do they need and value your expertise?
> Is their company culture capable of appreciating and trusting outside experts? It's not worth it to try and become a partner with a know-it-all.
> The amount of additional sales opportunities (obviously).
> Can you gain access to C-level decision makers and maintain that access over time?

Planning for Strategic Partner Relationships

To help you develop a plan for cultivating a strategic partner relationship, think of the matches between your selling team and the customer's buying and implementation teams, as shown in Table 11-1.

Table 11–1 Planning the Links with a Strategic Partner

CLIENT'S TEAM	C-LEVEL ("CHIEF" OR EXEC VP)	DIVISION MANAGER/VP	FUNCTIONAL DEPT MANAGER(S)	INTEGRATOR/ TECHNICAL EXPERT
Sales Team Exec Sponsor / VP of Mktg or Sales	X			
Regional Sales Mgr		X	X	
Account Manager	X	X	X	X
Implementation Support (IT, engineering, etc.)			X	X
Director of Customer Service			X	

Suppose you are selling financial software for enhancing and improving accounts receivable and accounts payable functions. Here's how you might structure a relationship:

- You want your C-level to contact their C-level. In this example, your SVP of sales would contact the customer's CFO.

- Your regional sales manager would be responsible for keeping in touch with the customer's finance manager.

- Your account manager, by definition, wants to have a relationship with everybody. So the account manager would want to go along if the SVP of sales meets the CFO, sit in on sessions between the regional sales manager and financial manager, and have direct relationships with both the accounts payable and accounts receivable managers.

- If the customer has concerns about compatibility, you'd want someone from your company with deep technical knowledge to be seen as a first line of support for either the functional managers and/or the technical experts inside the customer company.

The point of thinking through these options is so you can develop a plan for keeping in touch with your customers. Nothing can harm your credibility more than having multiple people contact the same customer employee about issues—it wastes their time (and yours), and it makes you look uncoordinated.

Getting More Referrals and Testimonials

If you have created a satisfied, loyal customer, you can often leverage that success to get more business.

For many salespeople, attempting to obtain referrals can be frustrating and unproductive. Customers often provide either poor referrals or none at all. Many salespeople underestimate the risk that buyers feel when they're asked to supply referrals: you're asking your customer to put their personal credibility on the line. Another difficulty is that your customer may not know the specific needs of their associates.

The first step for getting more referrals is to **ask at the right time.** Traditional sales training techniques usually teach salespeople to ask for referrals at the close of a sale, but that's too soon. It's another form of selling too fast. Your new customers haven't yet achieved value, and you are, in effect, asking them to send you off in another direction (selling to another customer) at the precise moment when they need you the most! At best, your request for a referral will be ignored. At worst, the trust you have worked so hard to build may be damaged. **The key is to ask for a referral after value has been achieved.** Help your customers through Step 7 (*Expectations of Value*) and make sure your customers are satisfied *before* asking for referrals.

Second, you need to **ask in the right way.** First, upon winning a sale, get connected to your new customer on LinkedIn. Then, after your customer's expectations of value have been achieved, ask for referrals to specific people your customer is connected to. When asking for referrals, you could say, "Mr. Customer, I noticed that you're connected to Bob at XYZ Corp. Would there be any chance of you introducing me?"

Third, **ask the customer to reference common issues.** Make a list of the three most common objections you hear. Then think about which of your customers were able to resolve those issues, and try to get testimonial letters describing how those issues were resolved. Your goal should be to get specific testimonials that serve a purpose instead of nonspecific letters that simply say "atta-boy" or "atta-girl." Specificity is more compelling than generalities, and de-

---

Tip: Capturing Endorsements

When the customer says something positive to you about you or your company, respond, "I really appreciate you saying that. Any chance you could send that to me in a quick email?" (Be sure to tell your customer that you'll white out their email address before sharing their message with others.)

tails make an endorsement sound real. Specific testimonial letters are more persuasive: a customer could describe their original concern or objection, what helped them to overcome that concern or objection, what helped them to achieve the results being enjoyed now.

Your Final Role: Chief Satisfaction Officer

Keeping customers is the first principle of growing a business. You are your company's "Chief Satisfaction Officer," and you must do everything in your power to retain customers. The best way to keep a customer satisfied and loyal is to grow that customer. Just as the seasons turn for a farmer, so too for you in your role as Farmer. To grow your customer, move forward on the sales wheel and arrive where you began: the Student and Doctor roles (see Figure 11-4).

Figure 11-4 Continue the Cycle

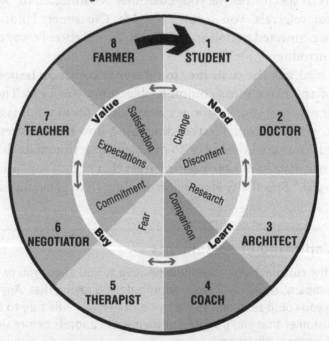

Continue to identify new needs and new areas
of discontent in your customers.

Study the new changes that are affecting your customers, and diagnose customers' problems triggered by those changes. You will create more satisfied customers if you continually look for new ways to add value to your customers. Chief Satisfaction Officers don't think "account maintenance," they think "account development."

Epilogue to Part II

Never before have your competitors been as strong, as fast, as hungry, or as agile as they are today. Never before have you faced as many *new* competitors as you do today. And they will be even more formidable tomorrow. So even if you are successful today, it's dangerous to assume you will *remain* successful simply by doing the same things that brought you success.

That's where the eight sales roles come in. By following the plan prescribed in this book, you will find numerous opportunities to sell more effectively and more strongly differentiate yourself from the competition. You will need to be persistent as you:

> Gain knowledge about a prospect's business. [Student]
> Explore the prospect's underlying needs, and the significance/priority of those needs. [Doctor]
> Shape a prospect's optimal solution design—the design that will achieve the most positive results for the client. [Architect]
> Communicate why your solution is each decision maker's best choice. [Coach]
> Resolve customer anxieties and concerns. [Therapist]

➢ Negotiate a win-win commitment. [Negotiator]

➢ Help your customer achieve maximum value. [Teacher]

➢ Create *satisfied* customers who become *loyal* to you and your company. [Farmer]

And woven throughout all of the above steps, you must always be aware of how the buying decision will be made, who are the members of the Complex Buying Team, and what the personal interests and needs of these multiple decision makers are.

As you become more comfortable using the techniques presented in the previous chapters, you'll find yourself again and again trying to get into your customer's head, and engaging in the buying process. You'll come to recognize the mistakes you made in the past when you jumped ahead in your selling process, only to leave your customer behind in their buying process.

Salespeople who are following this approach tell me that they get great satisfaction out of helping customers buy more effectively, and being able to better serve their customer's buying process. They know they can now differentiate themselves by the *way* they sell, not just *what* they sell. They see the value of spending more time with a customer prior to the buying decision because it creates stronger relationships, faster, and ultimately leads to greater sales and increased customer loyalty.

The days of moving too quickly through each sales conversation and missing opportunities to sell more effectively needs to become a thing of the past. That's my mission. Will you now make it yours?

Negotiate deals with commitment. [Negotiator]

PART III

Coaching the Eight Sales Roles

CHAPTER 12

Coaching for Success

Advice for Sales Managers
(and the People Who Work for Them)

Recently, in conjunction with an opportunity to deliver our sales management leadership workshop, I was retained by a Fortune 500 company to examine their job description for the sales manager position. Fully 85 percent of the duties were directly linked to *coaching* salespeople. (I've reviewed many sales manager job descriptions over the years, and this was one of the better ones.)

I then conducted face-to-face interviews with a number of the sales managers and found that less than 5 percent of their time was actually spent on coaching. Five percent! Another way to say this is that sales managers were spending 95 percent of their time focused on 15 percent of their job responsibilities. Why?

> ➤ Sales managers were spending three hours each day responding to about 150 emails, virtually none of which came from their sales team. Then there's the meetings, paperwork,

and fire-fighting. The list of "urgencies" for sales managers today is endless.

> These sales managers had been promoted to management because of their personal sales achievements. But they weren't trained on the *sales management* skills needed to develop an elite sales team. So they do what they feel comfortable doing—they keep selling, which doesn't develop their team.

During the course of my interviews I also spoke with a regional VP of sales, one level up from the sales manager position. I asked him what his theory was for achieving sales growth. His answer: "Keep my salespeople in the field as much as possible." To which I responded, "Why not apply the same theory to your sales managers, and try to keep *them* 'in the field' coaching as much as possible, too?"

In this chapter, I will share important tips and tools for coaching your salespeople in buying-focused selling. I'll first discuss the core issues around the type of sales coaching that is needed, and then provide suggestions on how to coach around the Milestones and the specific roles of the buying-focused selling process.

Tip: How Salespeople Can Use This Chapter

The best salespeople I know are, of course, open to learning from others. But they also learn by coaching themselves. They think about a sales call *before* they make it and afterwards take time to reflect on what happened: What went right? What could I have done differently? Though this chapter is written for sales managers, salespeople can use the tips and advice to help coach themselves and improve their sales skills.

What Is Coaching?

There are two types of sales coaching: performance management and developmental coaching. Performance management is the monthly or quarterly one-on-one meeting where you review a rep's sales results and judge their performance. Developmental coaching, on the other hand, is about developing the salesperson's competence and willingness to sell.

In short, performance management looks primarily to the past; developmental coaching looks to the future. Effective coaching consists of both performance management *and* developmental coaching.

The problem is that with all the distractions sales managers face, the first thing to go out the window is developmental coaching. You fall back on a quarterly performance review that for many of us has become more of a creative writing exercise. We haven't observed the salesperson selling, or intervened at milestones along the way, so when a sales rep is 75 percent of quota we're not sure why. **If**

Tip: Coaching the Roles Is Just *One* Component of Effective Sales Management

The lack of time for, and knowledge about, developmental coaching is just one challenge for the sales manager today. Going into details about the other challenges is beyond the scope of this book, but here's a list of the ten most common mistakes I see:

1. Failing to shift from "super salesperson" mode to managerial mindset.
2. Fighting fires continually.
3. Leaving your staff to sink or swim on their own.
4. Ignoring the importance of performance standards/getting blindsided by poor performance.
5. Failing to leverage the strengths and resources of your team's top producers.
6. Spending too much time working with the bottom 20 percent.
7. Allowing senior salespeople to get stuck in an unmotivated rut.
8. Being inconsistent in your recruiting and hiring process.
9. Assuming your sales reps will figure things out the same way you did.
10. Hanging on to low-producing salespeople for far too long.

To learn more, download my *free* whitepaper, "Overcoming the 10 Biggest Mistakes Sales Managers Make," at www.toplineleadership.com.

the only type of coaching we're doing is judgmental in nature, then salespeople don't think of it as coaching—they think of it as criticism. In contrast, if you are helping your sales reps think through what they need to do to win a sale and to improve their buying-focused selling skills, your interventions will be perceived as developmental coaching.

Telling Is Not Coaching

I'm sure you're familiar with the old sales axiom *telling is not selling*. Well, telling is not coaching either. Confucius had it right when he said, "What I hear I forget, what I see I may remember, but what I do I understand." He could have been talking to sales managers.

Learning hasn't occurred until the sales rep's behavior has changed. The best way for you to determine if your coaching is working is to observe the salesperson—hopefully in action on a series of sales calls with prospects. At the very least, you should participate in interactive role-playing in which you play the customer as the sales rep practices his or her skills. That will help you judge how well they interact with customers.

How to Improve Your Sales Coaching

As you start to build stronger skills around sales coaching, here are some key pointers:

Key #1: Get Involved Early in the Sales Process

Far too many sales managers get involved extremely late in the sales process, and even then they aren't coaching their salesperson, they are trying to negotiate and win the opportunity themselves. I have to wonder how much of a difference they can make because by that point the customer has already defined their needs and formulated a good idea of their solution. In addition, having the sales manager deal directly with the customer will likely diminish the salesperson's credibility, and sets the precedent in the customer's mind that they should always deal directly with the sales manager.

There are only three ways for your salespeople to increase sales: find more opportunities, increase their success rate of converting opportunities to sales, and increase the average dollar amount of each opportunity. For the customer, the size of the purchase is determined *early* in the buying process, not at the end. If you provide more coaching early on, you will help your reps make more sales and make larger sales.

I remember a workshop for salespeople where the audience had different levels of tenure and experience, including one recent new hire. At the beginning of the workshop I asked each participant to state what he or she wanted to take away. The new hire said, "I want to learn objection handling." I replied, "What you really want to learn is how to prospect. Because if you don't get the prospecting skills down, you won't get to the point where you need to handle objections." We need to think about coaching the same way.

"Well begun is half done" certainly applies to the sales management profession. Spend more time coaching the Student, Doctor, and Architect phases and less in the negotiation phase.

Key #2: Focus on Vital Issues

A common mistake sales managers make when coaching salespeople is to give them a laundry list of things they need to improve upon. Most of us only have the capacity to improve one or two things at any given time. You don't want to overwhelm your sales reps because you may damage their self-confidence. Not good.

Instead, you need to learn how to pick out the "vital few" most important things for each sales person to work on. Years ago I learned a great technique for diagnosing performance problems from *High Output Management*, the book by Andy Grove, former CEO of Intel. He advises us to write down both good points and bad points about an employee and look for *patterns* among all the items.[20] In this context, that would mean making a complete list of a sales rep's strengths and developmental needs, then looking at the whole thing and trying to **pick out the common threads** among all the items listed.

For example, suppose a rep's strength is a high amount of prospecting activity. But weaknesses include a low lead conversion rate and a low quote-to-close rate. What is a common link between those issues? Here's a hint: think about high prospecting activity as a warning sign of the rep's inability to make appointments. When viewed that way, I can think of at least four possible common threads:

1. The sales rep isn't asking second- or third-level diagnostic questioning. If not, why not?
2. The sales rep spends too much time talking about the exciting capabilities of your product/service, rather than focusing on underlying customer needs, problems, and solution criteria.
3. The salesperson lacks the self-confidence to engage C-level prospects in a thought-provoking way.
4. The salesperson lacks basic business acumen and is unable to connect with customers around their operational, strategic, or performance issues.

You would have to ask more questions and perhaps observe the rep in action to decide which of these issues is the root cause. But doing so has a higher payoff than trying to attack any of the weaknesses alone. **Coaching** *symptoms* instead of underlying causes does more harm than good. Accurate diagnosis of a performance problem means looking for the common threads, then applying a bit of detective work to consider:

- Is this a skill problem? If so, teach the skill.
- Is this a willingness/motivation problem? If so, help the rep understand the reasons why they need to improve.
- Is this a self-confidence problem dealing with C-level prospects? If so, encourage and coach the rep. Have them take a training program to improve their business acumen so they can converse with an executive in the executive's terms.

Key #3: Coach Slower So Salespeople Will Learn Faster

The following observation will not come as a big surprise by now: most sales managers **coach** too fast. When coaching, we don't help sales people find their own answers. We often don't listen to everything they want to tell us, but rather jump in with a diagnosis and prescription before they're done talking. Just as slowing down selling can help your customers buy faster, slowing down coaching can help your sales people learn faster!

One way to slow down so you get a better diagnosis of the key issues for each salesperson is to use the questioning approach described in the Doctor chapter. The purpose of the Doctor questioning was to help customers understand the nature and impact of their problems, so they can better judge what kind of solution they need. The same principle holds true when dealing with your sales reps: they have problems in their sales skills, but often don't fully understand the underlying causes nor the impact on customers and the probability of sales success. So when you're engaged in a coaching discussion, think like a Doctor to probe for a better understanding of underlying causes, not just symptoms. It only takes three simple steps:

Step #1: Identify the Situation and Symptoms

- What is the prospect's situation?
- Where are they in the buying process? How can you tell?
- Ask questions related to the specific step. For example, if the sales rep says the customer is in the *Research* step, you would ask, "What are their must-have and nice-to-have buying criteria?"

Step #2: Diagnose the Cause

- If you agree with the sales representative's analysis, go on. If not, dig deeper to diagnose why the salesperson doesn't accurately understand the situation. Is it a lack of knowledge or skill? Or perhaps a willingness problem?

> Use the Andy Grove method: list both strengths and weaknesses and look for patterns common to both the salesperson's strengths and weaknesses.

Step #3: Determine Alternatives and Next Steps

> Take at least one action related to advancing the sales opportunity.

> Take at least one action to develop/improve the sales representative's skills.

Getting the Most Value Out of Each Milestone

The Milestones identified in the book are built-in coaching points you can use in addition to the general developmental coaching described above. The basic approach to coaching the Milestones is based on an understanding of what salespeople should be learning as they facilitate the customer's buying process.

Your role is to review the salesperson's work and ask questions that he or she should know by that Milestone. If the salesperson can't answer your questions, or if the answers you hear are non-specific, this would suggest that the salesperson didn't ask the customer the right questions. If that's the case, ask the salesperson how he or she can get the answers to questions they can't answer now, and how they can do better at the pre-milestone steps the next time around. If the salesperson *can* answer your questions, your job is to make sure that they express their knowledge persuasively (in letters, MOUs, sales presentations, etc.).

Here are some specific issues to address in your one-on-ones for each Milestone.

Coaching Milestone #1: Getting More First Appointments

Early in my sales career I went through a period where I suffered an appointment-setting slump. Whereas I had been successful getting appointments in the past, suddenly my calendar was empty and I couldn't get any appointments. The harder I tried the worse success

I had. Then my sales manager listened to a few calls and quickly pinpointed my mistake: I was not asking often enough for the appointment. Earlier, in Chapter 4, I outlined the "CPA" method for telephone prospecting: Courtesy–Problem–Action. My "C" and "P" were good, but I had forgotten about "A," asking for action. Once my sales manager pointed this out I corrected the problem and my calendar filled up with more appointments.

I knew how to perform the task, I had done it effectively before. Then I hit a slump but was unable to self-diagnose my problem. This is a crucial contribution you can make as a sales coach—helping your salespeople remember what they already know.

If one of your salespeople is struggling to make appointments, chances are he or she is forgetting something they already know. Take another look at Milestone #1 (pages 70–82). Prospecting is not that difficult a skill to learn. Get involved with your salesperson: observe, assess, and then help them make the changes they need to make.

In my experience, there is no better way to coach telephone skills than to listen to tapes of actual prospecting calls. It's *efficient* because you don't have to sit next to the salesperson while they're making the calls, especially since so many calls have to be made before someone actually answers. You can listen to ten prospecting calls in less than twenty minutes. It's *effective* because you can hear both what your salesperson said and how the prospect responded.

Be sure to contact your company's HR department and ask if it is legal in your area to record a sales prospecting call for coaching purposes. While the U.S. federal law only requires one-party consent, many states have accepted different laws. To see the law in your state, visit http://www.callcorder.com/phone-recording-law-america.htm#State %20Laws%20(Table).

Coaching Milestone #2: Creating Momentum with a Memo of Understanding (MOU)

Coaching the MOU is without a doubt the most important coaching point in the buying process. If the salesperson meets with the customer the first time and is unable to answer key questions about the customer's needs, then there is no reason to work with this person on sales presentation skills! That's not the problem.

Here are the top five things to look for in an MOU:

1. Is it written in the customer's terms, rather than in your company's jargon? It should not sound like your brochure.

2. Does it clearly define the customer's problems and/or opportunities? Does it explain why the problem exists or what opportunity is facing the customer?

3. Does it identify some ripple effects and costs (to the customer) of doing nothing?

4. Is it short and succinct—not wordy?

5. Does it include a specific go-forward commitment (see pages 53–55) for the customer?

Coaching Milestone #3: Winning Presentations and Proposals

Here's a checklist you can use to evaluate and help improve a salesperson's presentation or proposal:

➢ Does it communicate all of our unique strengths?

➢ Does it differentiate us from the competition?

➢ Does it include information suitable for each key decision-maker group involved in the purchasing decision?

➢ Does it succinctly describe the customer's needs and tangible buying criteria?

➢ Does it include a justification for the investment?

➢ Does it include useful visuals?

➢ Does it have an attention-getting opening?

➢ Does it end with an example of a detailed implementation plan from another company?

Coaching Milestone #4: Transitioning from Pre- to Post-Sale

In many companies, the first action after a sale is confirmed is a handoff from the salesperson to an account manager or implementation support team. As the sales manager, it is your job to make sure this handoff goes smoothly. You don't want to fumble at this stage.

If you are responsible for supervising the transition and/or the first stages of implementation, a key coaching point is to focus on the draft implementation plan. Though the draft is a starting point for a collaborative effort with the customer, you can help it become as strong as possible by:

- Making sure that the plan identifies a project manager at your end.

- Asking the salesperson if he or she anticipates any challenges with the client's project manager.

- Reviewing what the salesperson *thinks* the customer's expectations are. Use your experience to gauge whether the expectations are realistic and achievable. If not, ask the salesperson to explain the plan for managing those expectations during the meeting with the customer's project manager.

- Asking the salesperson to describe whether there will be additional people involved in the implementation who were not involved in the buying decision. If so, what are their concerns/needs?

- Determining who needs to establish/maintain contact with any individuals on the original buying team (such as the Power Broker, a Super User, etc.).

- Asking the salesperson if he or she has given any thought to a strategy for measuring value.

Coaching the Sales Roles

I've found that coaching at the milestones of the sales process provides the most leverage, so those are the first places to focus your time and attention. However, your sales representatives will likely need help shifting from their old sales behaviors to the new customer-focused strategies described in this book. Use the buy-learning process during one-on-ones to improve mutual understanding. Show the salesperson a copy of the buying process wheel (Figure 1-2 on

Tip: Look for Go-Forward Commitments After Each Contact

A common problem for salespeople that I've talked about throughout the book is getting "go-forward" commitments (specific actions the customer commits to take). As a coach, you need to ask your salesperson what *actions* the customer has taken. **What's important is not where your salesperson is in his or her selling process, but where the customer is in their buying process.** The actions customers have taken tell you where they're at in the buying process.

page 10), and ask the sales rep, "Who are the players and what step of their buying process are they in?"

Other common challenges salespeople experience at each stage of the sales process and how you can help mitigate the problem as a coach are summarized in Table 12-1.

Table 12-1 Coaching the Sales Roles

ROLE	PROBLEM	COACHING HELP YOU CAN OFFER
Student	The sales representative is not comfortable approaching Core-level or C-level decision makers.	Select a prospect account and have the sales representative create a CPA statement (pp. 73–76 in Chapter 4) for a Core-level contact in that business. Review and role-play with the sales representative.
	The sales representative does not handle telephone objections well.	Have the representative develop responses to the most typical objections he/she hears. Role-play with them until they are comfortable responding to those objections.
Doctor	The sales representative is unsure of what potential issues to probe.	Have the sales representative create a list of potential solutions your company provides and develop a list of customer problems that a prospect might experience that would lead him or her to consider your solutions. Have the salesperson shape questions around these potential issues.

Table 12-1 *(continued)*

ROLE	PROBLEM	COACHING HELP YOU CAN OFFER
Doctor	The sales representative is not asking the right diagnostic questions of the customer.	Ask the salesperson to answer questions aligned to the structure of an MOU. For example, "What are two problems this customer has that we can solve? What are the causes of each problem? What are the ripple effects and costs should the customer decide to do nothing about the problems?" Whatever questions the salesperson can't answer are the questions that he or she should ask the prospect in the very next meeting.
Architect	The sales representative is unable to project what a prospect's must-have buying criteria might be.	Have the sales representative list all of your company's strengths in a column on the left side of a piece of paper, then to the right of each one, list the buying criteria that would support that strength. Review the list and suggest revisions as necessary. This can be done for a specific account or, if you feel that broader development is needed, for your company in general.
Coach	You're concerned the sales representative is unprepared for an important sales presentation.	Ask the following questions: What is your understanding of the customer's buying criteria? Which of these represent a competitive edge for us? Which of these represent a competitive disadvantage for us? Who is positioned most favorably at this time, you or a competitor? What can you do to influence the customer's criteria so that they see a better match between their needs and our offering? What are three reasons this customer should buy from us? (Listen for a connection between each of your company's strengths and an explicit customer need.)
Therapist	The salesperson does not have a strategy for dealing with the inevitable *Fear* stage.	Have your salesperson make a list of the typical fears experienced by your customers. Ask the salesperson, "What actions can you take or what information can you provide that will alleviate these fears?"

Table 12-1 *(continued)*

ROLE	PROBLEM	COACHING HELP YOU CAN OFFER
Negotiator	The sales representative does not prepare well for the negotiation.	Have the sales representative create a range of flexibility for each negotiable item. Also ask the sales rep to think of possible high-value, low-cost concessions that could be included in a negotiation other than a price reduction.
Teacher	The sales representative does not set performance expectations with the customer to measure the success of the solution.	Have the representative develop a list of the potential benefits your solution brings to a given customer. Next to each item have him or her list ways that those benefits can be observed and measured by the customer.
Farmer	The sales representative is not conducting Account Reviews or is conducting them poorly.	Arrange to have the sales representative attend an Account Review with another representative who does them particularly well.

Developing Salespeople's Complex Sales Skills

Another area for coaching that spans the entire sales process is making sure that your salespeople are continually developing their skills for dealing with Complex Buying Teams. Some examples are given in Table 12-2.

Your Mission: Create a Great Sales Team

Your role as a sales manager is not to do all the selling. Your role is to develop an elite, high-performance sales team. Coach your sales people to continually get better at helping their customers buy. To do that, you need to focus more on developmental coaching throughout the complete sales process, not just at the end (to "close" the deal) when any intervention from you will be too little, too late. Early intervention focused on effective application of the eight sales roles is how you can transition from being a stellar salesperson to a leader who has created a great sales *team*.

Now, lead the way!

Table 12-2 Typical Problems with Complex Sales Skills

SYMPTOM	ACTION(S)
The sales rep is spending too much time with only one decision maker.	Make sure the rep understands the importance of reaching multiple decision makers. Ask to see their 3x3 prospecting plan (see pp. 99–100 in Chapter 5). Question the sales rep about how they plan to get the second and third decision makers involved.
A sales rep is repeatedly stymied by Gatekeepers.	Once a Gatekeeper has been assigned, do not let the rep go around him or her. Work with the salesperson so that this problem is less of an issue in future sales opportunities. First, engage in more pre-call planning with the sales rep. Help him or her make a list of questions that the person they are going to meet with likely can't answer, and role-play how they should ask the contact to refer them to someone who can answer those questions.
A sales rep fails to reach the ROI Authority or Power Broker.	The salesperson is probably not getting in on the sales opportunity soon enough. This may be more of a prospecting problem. If the opportunities largely come about because customers contact him or her, then the salesperson is getting involved late in the buying process, after the ROI Authority has backed out and delegated the buying process to others. Somebody else has the ear of the Power Broker.

Endnotes

1. HR Chally Group, *The Chally World Class Sales Excellence Research Report* (Dayton, Ohio: HR Chally, 2006), p. 75.

2. Steven Covey, *The 7 Habits of Highly Effective People* (New York: Simon & Schuster, 1989, 2004), p. 233.

3. Frederick E. Webster and Yoram Wind, *Organizational Buying Behavior: Foundations of Marketing* (Englewood Cliffs, N.J.: Prentice Hall, 1972), p. 113. You may have to scour secondhand bookstores or go to the library on this one, but it will be worth your while.

4. John O'Shaughnessy, *Why People Buy* (New York: Oxford University Press, 1987).

5. Covey, *7 Habits*, p. 237.

6. Harvard Business Review, *Business Classics: Fifteen Key Concepts for ManagerialSuccess.* (Boston: Harvard Business School Publishing Corporation, 1991), pp. 51–57.

7. Michael M. Lombardo and Robert W. Eichinger, *FYI: For Your Improvement: A Guide for Development and Coaching*, 4th edition (Minneapolis, Minn.: Lominger International, 2006), p. 8.

8. Nicholas A. C. Read and Stephen J. Bistritz, *Selling to the C-Suite: What Every Executive Wants You to Know About Successfully Selling to the Top* (New York: McGraw-Hill, 2010), p. 9.

9. Read and Bistritz, *Selling to the C-Suite*, pp. 84, 85.

10. Paul Ekman and Wallace V. Friesen, *Unmasking the Face: A Guide to Recognizing Emotions from Facial Clues* (Cambridge, MA: Prentice-Hall, 1975).

11. Paul Nutt, *Why Decisions Fail: Avoiding the Blunders and Traps That Lead to Debacles* (San Francisco: Berrett-Koehler Publishers, 2002), p. ix.

12. Keith Eades, *The New Solution Selling: The Revolutionary Sales Process That Is Changing the Way People Sell* (New York: McGraw-Hill. 2004), p. 138.

13. Covey, *7 Habits*, p. 101.

14. David G. Ullman, *Making Robust Decisions: Decision Management for Technical, Business, and Service Teams* (Victoria, B.C., Canada: Trafford Publishing, 2006), p. 175.

15. Thomas F. Crum, *The Magic of Conflict: Turning a Life of Work into a Work of Art.* (New York: Touchstone/Fireside {Simon & Schuster}, 1987), pp. 40–48.

16. Theodore Levitt, *The Marketing Imagination* (New York: The Free Press, 1983, 1986), p. 111.

17. Chally Group, *Sales Excellence Research Report*, p. 3.

18. Dale Carnegie, *How to Win Friends and Influence People* (New York: Simon & Schuster, 1936, 1964).

19. Fred Reichheld. *The Ultimate Question: Driving Good Profits and True Growth.* (Boston: Harvard Business School Publishing Corporation, 2006).

20. Andrew S. Grove, *High Output Management* (New York: Vintage Press {Random House}, 1983, 1995), pp. 191–192.

Index

About the Author

Kevin Davis is the president of TopLine Leadership Inc., a sales and sales management training company based in Reno, Nevada, that serves clients from diverse sectors. Kevin's expertise is built on a 30+ year career in sales, sales training, and sales consulting. Along the way, he has personally observed tens of thousands of sales calls. In *Slow Down, Sell Faster!*, Kevin doesn't simply suggest *what* you need to do to be more buyer-focused, he also shares a multitude of anecdotes that describe the *how*.

In addition to running his company, Kevin keeps in touch with sales professionals via forums such as two-day workshops, half-day sales seminars and keynote speeches. He talks with several thousand sales professionals every year, which allows him to keep a pulse on issues important to sales managers and their teams.

Kevin has served on the front-lines of the sales profession and brings real-world experience to this book. He began his career with Lanier Worldwide, a Fortune 200 office equipment company, where he worked as a sales representative, major account executive, sales manager, and district general manager. While there, he earned the Chairman's Council award, presented annually to producers ranking in the top five percent. He also earned Lanier's prestigious "District Manager of the Year" Award. As a sales manager, Kevin hired, trained and coached over 250 salespeople.

Kevin's first book was *Getting Into Your Customer's Head: 8 Secret Roles of Selling Your Competitors Don't Know* (Times Business/Random House). It was voted one of the top 30 business books of 1996 by

Soundview Executive Book Summaries (out of 1,500 titles considered annually).

Kevin's formal education includes a B.A. in Business Administration from California State University-Chico, and extensive postgraduate work at U.C. Berkeley on the subject of instructional design. Kevin and his wife, who have two children, live in the Reno-Tahoe area.

You can reach Kevin through his company's website: www .toplineleadership.com. TopLine Leadership Inc. (located in Reno, Nevada) provides the skills and tools that sales-driven companies need to create elite, high-performance sales teams. It offers two types of training and coaching available in formats including open enrollment, in-house custom and train-the-trainer:

➤ It trains salespeople to outsell competitors by slowing down each sales conversation and becoming more focused on the customer's buying cycle throughout their sales process.

➤ Its Sales Management Leadership workshop combines how-to skills such as sales coaching, communicating, and motivating teams with the self-management skills that will help them free up more time for sales coaching.

TopLine Leadership has been in business since 1989 helping clients achieve a much greater level of sales competitiveness. Past and current clients include successful corporate sales organizations, including major multinational corporations and small and medium-sized firms, including start-up and growth-oriented firms.

Its clients have come from many different sectors including software, document management, transportation/logistics, business services, career/staffing services, financial services, professional services, wireless, telecom, healthcare, manufacturing, heavy equipment, and media.

CPSIA information can be obtained
at www.ICGtesting.com
Printed in the USA
LVHW040153260619
622364LV00008B/129/P

9 780814 416853